Quick and Easy

CHINESE
COOKING

Printed for Hoan Products, Ltd.
L.I.C., N.Y.   11101

Quick and Easy

CHINESE
COOKING

BY KENNETH H. C. LO
with decorations by Bobby Altman

HOUGHTON MIFFLIN COMPANY BOSTON

Fourth printing w

First American edition 1972

ISBN: 0–395–13523–0
Library of Congress Catalog Card Number: 70–151463
Printed in the United States of America

Foreword

ALL THE RECIPES in this book are either quick to cook or easy to cook, or both.

Those which are quick to cook you will find also quite simple to prepare. On the other hand, those which are simple to prepare are not necessarily also quick to cook; indeed, some of these may require more than one hour to cook, or even two hours. However, in these cases, the amount of work actually involved in the cooking is often minimal, probably involving no more than putting a casserole in the oven or placing a heavy pan over low heat and leaving it there till the food inside is ready. Because such cooking requires little or practically no attention, the total consumption of energy in these cases is often less than in others where the preparation and cooking time together do not add up to ten minutes. For this reason I often recommend that a Chinese meal of four or five dishes include one or two long-cooked dishes which will mature on their own while the host or hostess can attend to the quick-cooked ones. In this way, by reducing the number of things one has to do at a given time, a multidish dinner can be prepared at a leisurely pace. Once you have achieved the rhythm of preparing a Chinese meal at a measured and leisurely pace, you have more than half won the battle — if it can be so described!

Because of too much straining for authenticity and atmosphere, many excellent Chinese cookery books published in recent years have inadvertently contributed to a deepening of the mystique which surrounds this subject. I hope that the contents of this book will help dispel something of this mystique. After all, anything which can be done both quickly and easily from quite ordinary materials cannot be too mystical! Many subjects which have a vast historical, regional and classical background can by their sheer size and antiquity generate a cloud of mythology around them. These subjects often deserve bringing down to earth and debunking. Chinese food and cooking are no exception.

I hope these dishes — undemanding as most of them are — will tempt the reader to try his hand at a style of cuisine which can honestly be described as fun, and which is at the same time highly various, economical and extremely tasty.

KENNETH H. C. LO

Contents

viii CONTENTS

Quick and Easy

CHINESE
COOKING

1

Basic Ingredients

MANY PEOPLE appear to have the impression that it is necessary to use a great many rare and exotic materials and ingredients in Chinese cooking. This is not so at all. The food materials used in Chinese cooking are for all practical purposes the same as those used in the Western style (the exceptions which exist merely prove the rule). As for flavoring and seasoning ingredients, so long as you have soy sauce, which is obtainable almost anywhere these days, you can cook Chinese. All the other ingredients and seasonings used are similar to or the same as those normally used in Western cooking, such as salt, pepper, chili powder, mustard, garlic, onion, spring onion (scallion), parsley, chives. An exception such as root ginger can be replaced by chopped lemon- or orange-peel shavings.

Some other ingredients and seasonings which would be useful to have around when you intend to cook Chinese include:

> Cornstarch
> Dry sherry
> Tabasco
> Tomato sauce or tomato purée
> Gelatin
> Pickles and chutneys
> Beef and chicken stock cubes or powder

If convenience foods or frozen foods are admissible in good Western cooking, they can certainly also be incorporated in good Chinese cooking, provided they are pepped up with a proportion of fresh foods at crucial points in the process.

2

Kitchen Equipment
and Methods

MANY PEOPLE SUPPOSE that to practice Chinese cooking one would require a whole range of Chinese equipment and kitchen utensils. Not at all. One can cook Chinese without the use of any of the typically Chinese equipment. I have done so for years. The equipment of a modern kitchen is quite capable of coping with all forms and style of Chinese cooking, and may indeed have many advantages over the typical Chinese kitchen; if well used it should considerably speed up the whole cooking process. This is not to say that there are not some items in use in the Chinese kitchen which are immensely effective. The razor-sharp chopper, the half-foot-thick tree-trunk chopping board, the round-bottom smooth-contoured frying pan (the wok) and the multilayer bamboo basket steamer all have their strong points but unless you are well-practiced in their uses their presence would contribute more to the rustic effect than to general efficiency.

In the modern kitchen there are the refrigerator and the oven, often both lacking in the old Chinese kitchen. Then there are the grill, the revolving spit, the electric mixer, the pressure cooker, even the mechanical cutter (useful for thin slicing) and above all the can opener, all of which can be used to advantage.

The only things you would really need to start cooking Chinese are a couple of saucepans and frying pans. However, it would be an advantage to have a frying pan with a lid, as sometimes when you introduce wet materials into a very hot pan with oil you may need to shield yourself with the lid. Also, in Chinese "stir-frying," you would quite often introduce a few spoonfuls of broth and close the lid for a couple of minutes of braising under cover before starting another session of final stir-fry.

As for saucepans, it would be useful to possess at least one heavy one, or an iron pot, which could be used for long-simmering. The wide variety of heavy casseroles which are currently available should come in handy, for cooking on the range or for long-simmering in the oven.

One type of cooking practiced widely in China is steaming. It would be useful, therefore, to have a steamer, particularly an oval-shaped or elongated one, so that a whole fish can be cooked in it. Lacking this, one can always convert any large saucepan into a steamer simply by placing food to be cooked in a deep-sided heatproof dish or basin and standing it in a saucepan containing about one inch of water. When the water is brought to a boil the food in the dish will be steamed. The only thing one has to be careful about is not to allow any of the water in the pan to slosh into the dish containing the food. When a comparatively shallow heatproof dish is used, it will have to be set on a platform above the boiling water. This can be achieved by placing two or three eggcups or some other suitable object at the bottom of the pan.

In the case of long-steaming in China, the dish containing the food is usually closed; "closed steaming" is really equivalent to double-boiling and can in fact be done in a double boiler.

Otherwise, the only thing you will require to get started is a good long-handled metal spoon for stir-frying. Other accessories useful to have are a collection of bowls, saucers and small dishes for the various ingredients and cut-up materials to be apportioned into when preparing food for cooking.

Stir-frying

Although over the whole range of Chinese cooking there are at least forty-nine established methods of heating, which I have discovered and listed in another book, the only method which a Westerner will have to learn in Chinese cooking is "stir-frying" (sometimes known as "quick-frying," or — to give a graphic description of what actually happens — "quick-stir-frying"). Of the other forty-eight methods many are in common use in the West — deep-frying, grilling, roasting, etc.

— but the bulk of them are preoccupied with delicate opera-
tions of controlled acceleration and deceleration of heating,
such as cooking in "receding heat," or by rapid reduction of
liquid, or more or less use of water, wine, oil at different stages
of heating. I do not feel that preoccupation with these fancy
methods, no matter how time-honored and established, will
add much to one's initial mastery of Chinese cuisine. But the
practice and acquaintance with stir-frying (short for quick-
stir-frying) is a must.

Stir-frying is in its essence very simple. It involves heating
a small quantity of oil or fat (usually not much more than 2
or 3 tablespoons) in a frying pan with a lid or a saucepan —
the latter splashes less. When the oil becomes very hot, as it
does within seconds, the meat and other food materials are
added and are stirred together. These meats and materials
have generally been cut into very thin slices, or shredded into
matchstick-thin strips, or diced into ¼-to-¾-inch cubelets.
These materials are usually stirred in the hot oil for a few seconds to 3 or 4 minutes, with a metal spoon or bamboo chopsticks, then they are removed and put aside. A further small
quantity of oil (about 1 tablespoon) is often added to the pan,
followed by the other constituents of the dish — often dried
or fresh vegetables, also reduced to thin slices, shreds or small
cubes — for a short period of frying (a few seconds to 2
minutes). In the final phase the meat is returned to the pan for
an "assembly frying" with all the other materials. This final
stir-frying generally does not last for more than a minute, and
often at this stage a small amount of chicken broth and wine
or sherry are added, with the beneficial effect of preventing
scorching as well as providing some gravy for the dish. Sea-

sonings can often be adjusted at this stage, and not infrequently cornstarch (blended in double its amount of water) is added, especially when there is ample gravy; and in some instances a drop or two of an aromatic oil (such as sesame oil) at the last moment will add to the fragrance of the dish (in the West a drop or two of liqueur might help to add appeal).

In cooking vegetables, fish or other seafoods, a small amount of chopped spring onion (scallion) and garlic (crushed and chopped) and ginger root where available are usually introduced and fried in hot oil for about half a minute before the main foods are added. If you impregnate the oil first with these strong vegetables, and lubricate the main foods with it, the appeal of the dish is often heightened and overfishiness or any other unwanted taste or smell is suppressed.

It should be noted that when food materials are cut into very small or thin pieces, under the action of hot oil, even pork can be well cooked within 3 or 4 minutes. Beef and chicken can often be cooked in under half a minute (depending partly on quantity of food and size of pan), and soft vegetables in 1 to 2 minutes. If anything is suspected of being slightly undercooked, adjustment can usually be made, as with seasonings, in the final assembly frying. Quite often foods will cook to some extent in their own heat, while waiting for this final session of cooking. There appears to be plenty of margin for adjustments in all stages of the procedure, which is what makes Chinese cooking so flexible. When all the actions are carried out with rapidity and rhythm, stir-frying is like conducting an orchestra. The chef "orchestrates" the flavors and the heat and demonstrates his virtuosity. But it is a form which the average Westerner will require some practice to get used to.

The stirring in "stir-fry" is simply the action of stirring, turning, scrambling, and occasionally tossing (here one has to be careful) food materials in hot oil, so that all parts of the food are evenly covered and their contact with the hot pan is rotated and evenly maintained. This assures that the foods are quickly and evenly done, under the cook's very eyes.

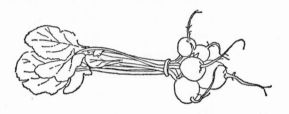

3

How Easy? Broths and Sauces

INDIVIDUAL CHINESE DISHES can often be prepared and cooked very quickly — in a matter of a few minutes. But a proper Chinese meal is a communal meal, cooked and served for the whole family, or a group — at least three or four people. Such a meal should consist of a minimum of three or four dishes, in addition to rice and soup. Because of this multiplicity of dishes, a typical Chinese meal will consume time to prepare and cook.

Two things greatly reduce the time in Chinese cooking: cooking several dishes at once, a habit which comes easily, and the practice of having all the necessary foods and made-up ingredients ready beforehand, which again one falls into naturally as one goes along. Both of these habits are ingrained in Chinese cooks.

If one were to start from scratch, without any of the foods and ingredients prepared or concocted, a meal of three dishes with soup and rice might require an hour or more to prepare. But if some of the foods can be prepared at moments of leisure, and some of the ingredients made up and laid out beforehand, and if, wherever possible, the dishes are cooked simultaneously, the time required can be easily reduced by half.

In a professional Chinese kitchen, where everything is ready and on hand, one often sees the speed of cooking rising up not just to four-minute dishes, but very often to "minute a dish," and occasionally, when several frying pans are working at a feverish speed at the same time, the speed may rise to the incredible rate of four dishes a minute!

But with us ordinary mortals, who should be content with producing a dish every 10 to 15 minutes, the time required for preparing and cooking a soup, rice and three dishes may well be contracted to under 30 minutes for anyone who has had a couple of run-throughs of the procedure.

For instance, in preparing such a meal, the rice and soup can usually be started first on the two back burners, leaving the two front burners for cooking and frying up the meat dish and vegetable dishes, while the oven can be used to cook the third savory dish. Here one has simply to calculate so that all the dishes will mature at the same time.

When you have got the soup and rice started, and the third dish inserted in the oven, you will only have the meat dish and the vegetable dish to deal with. Since vegetables seldom take more than 5 minutes to cook, and meat which has been sliced, shredded or diced seldom takes more than 6 or 7 minutes, if you were to apportion 15 minutes to cook these two dishes separately or 10 minutes if you were to cook them simultaneously, you would have plenty of time. In fact you would be able to cook them at leisure.

For rice to be perfect you would only have to flush it with a cup of boiling water and leave the lid firmly closed, after it had absorbed all the initial water; turn off the heat altogether after 6 minutes of further low-fire simmering, and let the rice cook in its own heat. Four to five minutes later the rice is ready to serve whenever required. (See recipe for Boiled Rice on p. 42.) Soup is something which doesn't demand much looking after once it is started. It may need some slight seasoning adjustments or perhaps a few more ingredients dropped in, propelled by a stir or two. As for the dish in the oven, it only needs to be brought out when all the other dishes are ready for the table — so long as it was originally well seasoned, marinated and garnished.

On the other hand, if one is merely preparing a mixed meat dish with vegetables to serve on rice, as a kind of self-contained platter for a single person, then such a Chinese dish or meal can usually be knocked off in a matter of minutes.

Broths and Sauces

Chinese cooking can be made quicker and easier if a few composite materials which are constantly used are made up beforehand, so that they can be taken from the cupboard or refrigerator whenever required. There are only a few of these materials, and they can be made up from ingredients which are available everywhere today. These few standbys are:

Superior Broth
Gunpowder Sauce (this is what we Chinese use in
    almost every other dish)
Meat Gravy Sauce (a derivative of Gunpowder Sauce)
Fu Yung Sauce (White Sauce)
Sweet and Sour Sauce
Wine Sediment Paste
Plum Sauce

Broth (*Superior Broth*)

The Chinese Superior Broth, which we shall for convenience just call "Broth," is used in or added to almost all nonmeat dishes, including soup. Broth should be made as follows, and since you will need a reasonable amount for frequent use, we shall make 3 to 4 pints.

Half an old chicken (or meaty   4 pints water
    skeleton)   1 chicken stock cube
1½ pounds spareribs   ¼-pound piece of chicken

Simmer chicken in water with spareribs for 1¼ hours. Add chicken stock cube and piece of chicken and simmer for another half-hour. Remove all bones and meat (for other uses). Allow liquid to stand and cool. When cold skim away all fat and impurities. The Broth is ready and can be kept in the refrigerator for later use.

Simplified Broth

1 pound spareribs   6 cups water
1 piece chicken (¼ pound)   1 chicken stock cube

Simmer spareribs and chicken in water for 1 hour. Skim and add stock cube. This is a simpler form of Broth. Though not as highly recommended, it can be used in recipes where Broth is called for.

Gunpowder Sauce

I call it "Gunpowder Sauce" because it is the sauce which is chiefly responsible for the difference between Chinese and Western cooking. Except for the plain-cooked and white-cooked dishes, it is used in nearly all meat, poultry, fish and vegetable dishes. Normally one does not use a great quantity of it (in stir-fried dishes seldom more than 2 or 3 tablespoons), but it will be handy to keep at least half a pint on hand:

1 cup soy sauce   1 tablespoon chopped lemon-
4 tablespoons sherry   peel shavings (or 3 slices
½ cup Broth   ginger root if available)
1 tablespoon sugar   ½ chicken stock cube
1½ tablespoons chopped onion

Heat and simmer the above ingredients together for 15 minutes, stirring occasionally. Keep in a bowl for use.

Meat Gravy Sauce

1 pound pork or beef   1 pint Gunpowder Sauce
1½ pints water

This is a derivative of Gunpowder Sauce. It is simply a meatier version, which can be produced by simmering the pork or beef in water for 15 minutes, pouring away half the water, adding the Gunpowder Sauce and continuing to simmer over very low heat for 1 hour. Remove the meat (for other uses) and keep the gravy. This Meat Gravy Sauce is used extensively for cooking vegetables and fish, or it can be used in soups and pastas.

Fu Yung Sauce (*White Sauce*)

The principal difference between Chinese and Western white sauces lies in the Western use of milk, flour and butter, and the Chinese use of egg white, cornstarch, minced chicken and Broth (occasionally with white wine thrown in). If we could use both types of ingredients, we would have the best of both worlds. And why not? The best way to do this is probably as follows:

3 tablespoons butter   2 beaten egg whites
4 tablespoons flour   ½ teaspoon salt
6 tablespoons Broth   Pepper to taste
½ cup milk   3 tablespoons cream (or
4 tablespoons finely minced   evaporated milk)
   chicken

Heat butter and make a roux with flour, as you normally do in making a white sauce. Slowly pour in Broth and milk, stirring all the time. When that is well blended, add chicken, egg whites (beaten until almost stiff), salt and pepper.

Continue to stir, and finally add 3 tablespoons cream or evaporated milk. Stir until the white sauce is consistent. Dispense with minced chicken if too time-consuming.

This sauce can be used successfully with vegetables such as cauliflower, which have been prefried, or braised or cooked in Broth, often with chicken (boiled, long-simmered and sliced), or in mixtures of seafoods and diced chicken, in which case a small amount of white wine should be added.

This sauce is best used fresh but can be kept in the refrigerator for a day or two.

Sweet and Sour Sauce

This sauce is often made fresh when required, as it takes very little time to make and is simplicity itself. It is best used fresh. It is most often used on meat and fish, and sometimes on vegetables. It is occasionally pepped up, or hotted up, by adding a small amount of Tabasco or chili powder.

2 tablespoons sugar
1 tablespoon cornstarch, blended in 4 tablespoons water
2 tablespoons vinegar
2 tablespoons tomato purée
2 tablespoons orange or pineapple juice

2 tablespoons soy sauce
2 tablespoons sherry
1 pimento or sweet (green) pepper
1 or 2 tablespoons pickles (or mixed pickles)
2 tablespoons oil

Mix first seven ingredients in a bowl. Cut pimento or sweet pepper into thin slices, and chop pickles. Heat oil in a saucepan or frying pan. When hot add the pickles and pimento to stir-fry slowly together for 1 minute. Pour in the sauce mixture, and stir until the sauce thickens, when it will be ready for use.

Wine Sediment Paste

In China Wine Sediment Paste is made from the lees or dregs from the bottom of the wine jars. It is used with great success in cooking with meats, poultry, fish and other seafood, whether for frying, stewing or preserving. A version of it can be made as follows:

2 teaspoons ground rice
2 tablespoons onion, finely chopped
2 tablespoons tomato purée
2 cloves garlic, crushed and finely chopped
1 tablespoon capers, finely chopped

1½ tablespoons lemon-peel shavings, finely chopped
½ tablespoon sugar
½ teaspoon salt
2 tablespoons vegetable oil
1 tablespoon soy sauce
⅔ cup sherry
2 tablespoons brandy

Stir-fry the first eight ingredients together in oil in a small heavy saucepan over a moderate heat for 3 to 4 minutes. Add sherry and soy sauce. Stir with a wooden spoon until the volume is reduced to under half. Add 2 tablespoons brandy. Leave mixture to stand and cool.

This is very winy material. It is able to suppress or remove any unwanted flavors, such as overfishiness, or the peculiar taste one sometimes encounters in meats and game. When it is applied to lightly cooked foods, such as lightly boiled chicken or fish, it gives them a "drunken" effect and can preserve them for long periods of time in sealed jars.

Plum Sauce

1 pound plums (stones removed)	2 tablespoons sugar
1 cup water	4 tablespoons soy sauce

Simmer plums in water for ¾ hour and strain through sieve, then stir in sugar and soy sauce. Heat gently for another ¼ hour, stirring frequently or as required.

I hope I have not conveyed the impression that all these types of material should be made up before one even embarks on Chinese cooking. The fact is that they should be made ready only if there appears a good prospect of using them in the course of the week; often they can be made up during the day on which one is cooking, or even on the spot.

In the Chinese kitchen the only two items which are in constant readiness are the Broth and Gunpowder Sauce.

4

Menu-making and Portions

IN PLANNING a Chinese meal it is best to regard the meal as a buffet, where everybody helps himself from the spread of dishes on the table. As such, there should be at least three or four dishes on the table for the diners to help themselves from. These need to be increased only when it begins to appear that there is not enough food to go around, or, if there are guests, that there isn't sufficient appearance of generosity or largesse. As a rule a Chinese meal of three or four dishes is calculated for three or four persons. Should the number of diners increase by one or two, it is not always necessary to increase the number of dishes accordingly. If one or two of them are large dishes, as they often are, there can easily be sufficient food without making any increase in the number or size of the dishes.

The majority of Chinese long-cooked dishes of meat stew and poultry are large dishes, which if they are not completely consumed in one meal can be heated up again for another. Hence there are always one or two long-cooked dishes kept in readiness in the pantry. When these are supplemented by one or two quick-cooked dishes (usually stir-fried ones) plus a soup, you will have a complete, well-balanced Chinese meal ready and prepared all within perhaps a quarter of an hour. The soup, by the way, is treated as one item of the buffet and is left on the table to be drunk a mouthful or two at a time throughout the meal — in place of water or any other beverage.

What is a well-balanced Chinese menu? It is simply a menu with items which represent a good variety in materials, color and texture. For example, if you have a heavy, long-cooked meat dish, you will have a pure vegetable dish to balance it; the vegetable being green, fresh and crunchy, the meat being brown, rich and tender. To further balance the meal, you may have a fish or other seafood dish or boiled chicken or an egg dish; the egg being yellow, the fish and chicken white, the seafood pink. Their tastes too are very different or contrasting. On the other hand, if you do not have a rich brown meat dish to start with, and you are relying on a long-simmered poultry dish to provide the main meat content of the meal, you might prepare a large bowl of red-cooked cabbage with Meat Gravy Sauce, which possesses much of the rich brown quality of a long-cooked meat dish. Since the majority of Chinese meat or vegetable dishes are capable of numerous minor variations, there is never any lack of items to fill up the gap, depending on what is at hand. Then again, of course, it depends upon one's inclination: if inclined toward seafoods, one can have a shellfish dish in addition to a fish dish; and if inclined toward meat, after the main stewed meat dish, one can have a quick-fried meat dish. This would be made of either chopped, diced, sliced, shredded or minced meats, cross-cooked with vegetables particularly suitable for cooking with meats of a particular size and shape — minced meat with peas, shredded meats with shredded vegetables, large pieces of chopped meat with carrots or turnips, diced meats with nuts, etc. The possibilities here are quite limitless.

Portions: The recipes in this book are basically calculated for about four portions (unless otherwise specified), to be placed on the table along with three other dishes. There will be instances where there will be more food than can be consumed. In such cases, the leftovers can be kept in a refrigerator to be reheated and rearranged for another meal. To do this is very much in the tradition of Chinese cooking.

Suggested Menus

Here are four lots of suggested menus, oriented toward *meat, poultry, fish and other seafoods* and *vegetables.*

In those instances where there might appear to be insufficient food, my suggestion is to pick an easy dish from a section of the recipes which is not already represented in the menu and prepare it as a supplementary dish. Alternatively, if one dish has gone down particularly well, repeat the dish or make a similar one using slightly different material (instead of beef, use lamb; or, instead of celery, bean sprouts).

For those Westerners who intend to cook something simple for themselves or for just two persons, the best plan would be to stick to the rice and pasta dishes (Fried Rice, Topped Rice and Noodles) and to cook just one other dish — of a contrasting material. If the rice or noodles are topped or fried with pork, cook a seafood or chicken and mushroom dish to go along with it. To cater to such requirements, I have provided an additional set of menus, *Extra Quick and Easy Menus*.

It will be noted that plain boiled rice is eaten with the dishes of the first four types of menu; it is there to absorb some of the richness and provide the bulk. In the case of the fifth category, rice or pasta appears as the main constituent of one dish in a two-dish combination, so there is no necessity of providing any other bland food to offset what might have been oversavoriness. Soup is provided in all menus except the Extra Quick and Easy ones.

I have provided only a very limited number of sweets in this book, mainly because it is not the Chinese custom to serve desserts at mealtime. The four desserts at the end of the book and their possible variants will fit most menus, or any of the lighter Western desserts can be used to conclude a Chinese meal.

And for the type of wines to drink with Chinese meals? Chinese wines are as yet too difficult to obtain. The best

Western wines to drink with Chinese meals are all the light, dry, white wines — nothing sweet, heavy and rich, since most Chinese savory dishes already contain some elements of sugar. A sparkling wine is suitable for starting off a Chinese meal where hors d'oeuvres are served.

Meat-oriented
(*for four or five persons*)

Pork Spareribs and Cucumber Soup
Red-cooked Pork
Quick-fried Sliced Beef with Oysters
Plain-fried Spinach
Steamed Eggs
Boiled Rice

Lamb and Leek Soup
Quick-fried Ribbons of Beef with Bean Sprouts
White-cooked Pork
Triple-layer Scrambled Omelet with Shrimps
Red-cooked Cabbage
Boiled Rice

Sliced Beef with Tomato and Egg-flower Soup
Triple-quick-fries
Red-cooked Spareribs
Egg-flower Meat
Quick-fried White-braised Cauliflower
Boiled Rice

Sliced Pork and Mushroom Soup
Red-cooked Beef
Quick-fried Sliced Lamb with Young Leeks
Scrambled Omelet with Sweet and Sour Sauce
Quick-fried Broccoli in Fu Yung Sauce
Boiled Rice

Poultry-oriented

(for four or five persons)

Cream of Fish Soup with Shrimps
Chopped Red-cooked Chicken
Orange Duck
Pork-stuffed Eggs in Sweet and Sour Sauce
Quick-fried Braised Lettuce
Boiled Rice

Sliced Beef with Watercress Soup
Diced Chicken Quick-fried in Soy Sauce
Aromatic and Crispy Duck
Chinese Salad
Boiled Rice

Pork Spareribs and Celery Soup
Chopped Salted Deep-fried Chicken
Pan-roast Red-cooked Duck
Stir-fried Shredded Pork with Spring Onions
Red-cooked Celery
Boiled Rice

White Fish and Green Pea Soup
Diced Chicken Quick-fried in Hot Sauce
Clear-simmered Duck with Onions and Spring Greens
Quick-fried Shrimps (or Scallops) with Mushrooms
in Meat Gravy Sauce
Steamed Vegetable Bowl
Boiled Rice

Seafood-oriented

(for four or five persons)

Chinese Chicken Noodle Soup
Red-cooked Fish
Abalone Quick-fried with Mushrooms and Broccoli
Stuffed Sweet Peppers
Casserole of Cabbage and Brussels Sprouts with Pig's Trotters

Whitefish and Spring Green Soup
Plain Salted Double-fried Fish Steaks
Quick-fried Shrimps (or Giant Prawns) with Tomatoes
Steamed Minced Pork Pudding with Cauliflower
Boiled Rice

Lamb and Leek Soup
Sweet and Sour Carp
Quick-fried Crabs in Egg Sauce
Stir-fried Sliced Pork with Cabbage
Casserole of Celery and Watercress with Eel
Boiled Rice

Triple-shred Soup
Grilled Crabs
Clear-simmered Fish
Drunken Duck
Casserole of Leeks and Cabbage with Lamb Chops
Boiled Rice

Vegetable-oriented
(for four or five persons)

Vegetable Soup
Vegetarian Quick-fried Spinach
Red-cooked Cabbage
Crab Scrambled Omelet
Fish Steaks in Sweet and Sour Sauce
Diced Chicken with Sweet Pepper and Chili Pepper
Boiled Rice

Egg-flower Soup (Soup of the Gods)
White-cooked Celery
Casserole of Cabbage and Brussels Sprouts with Squabs
Plain Salted Double-fried Fish Steaks
Soy-simmered Hard-boiled Eggs
Boiled Rice

Green Jade Soup
Red-cooked Celery
Stir-fried Spinach with Shrimps
Red-cooked Fish Steaks
Chopped Braise-fried Chicken in Wine Sediment Paste
Boiled Rice

Green and White Soup
White-cooked Cabbage
Quick-fried Leeks or Sweet Peppers with Shredded Beef
Double-fried Eel
Fancy Steamed Eggs
Boiled Rice

Extra Quick and Easy Menus
(for one, two or three persons)

Rice-oriented

Meat Fried Rice
Quick-fried Sliced Lamb with Young Leeks

Seafood Fried Rice
Diced Chicken Quick-fried in Soy Sauce

Vegetable Fried Rice
Red-cooked Fish Steaks

Topped Rice with Diced Chicken, Mushrooms
and Frozen Peas
Quick-fried Shrimps (or Giant Prawns) with Tomatoes

Topped Rice with Sliced Soy Steak and Broccoli
Egg-flower Meat

Topped Rice with Sweet and Sour Pork
and Fu Yung Cauliflower
Stir-fried Spinach with Shrimps

Noodles-oriented

Chicken and Mushroom Chow Mein with Green Beans
or Pea Pods
Quick-fried Sliced Beef with Kidneys

Lamb and Leek Chow Mein
Stir-fried Pork with Bean Sprouts

Chow Mein with Shredded Duck and Celery
Diced Chicken Quick-fried with Cucumber
and Button Mushrooms

Gravy Noodles with Red-cooked Pork and Spinach
Shredded Chicken Quick-fried with Bean Sprouts

Gravy Noodles with Spiced Beef and Tomatoes
Sliced Chicken Quick-fried with Pig's Liver

Gravy Noodles with Chicken and Oyster
Triple-quick-fries with Wine Sediment Paste

5

Soups

BROTH (see recipe on page 12) is an essential component of Chinese soups. Indeed, it is the base of nearly all, whether they be meat, vegetable or fish soups, or made-up ones such as meat-and-vegetable soups, or the Hot and Sour Soup. In preparing soups, I must presume that the Broth is ready made.

Pork Spareribs and Cucumber Soup

1 pound spareribs	1 teaspoon salt
4 cups water	Pepper to taste
1 6-inch segment cucumber	½ tablespoon soy sauce
2 cups Broth	

Cut spareribs into individual ribs. Trim away any uneven or

fatty bits. Place in 4 cups water. Bring to boil and simmer for 30 minutes. Pour away half the water and skim away any impurities.

Clean cucumber thoroughly. Cut into 3 2-inch segments and cut each segment lengthwise into 8 strips. Add them to the saucepan together with Broth and salt and pepper. Simmer them together for 15 minutes, add soy sauce and serve in a large tureen or in individual bowls. Diners should be encouraged to pick up the ribs and chew them, after drinking up the soup.

Pork Spareribs and Celery Soup

Repeat the preceding recipe, using 3 large stalks of celery instead of cucumber. As with cucumber, add the celery to the soup to simmer with the spareribs approximately 15 minutes before serving.

Spareribs with Carrot and Turnip Soup

1 pound spareribs	¼ pound turnips
Ham bones, about ¾ pound	2 cups Broth
4 cups water	1 teaspoon salt
¼ pound carrots	Pepper to taste

Boil the spareribs and ham bones in water for 20 minutes; pour away half the water and remove ham bones.

Peel and discard any coarse parts of the vegetables and cut them into triangular wedge-shaped pieces using enough to make 1 cup of each. Add them to the spareribs together with Broth. Adjust for seasonings, simmer together for 45 minutes and serve.

Longer cooking time is required in this case to soften the hard vegetables as well as to tenderize the spareribs.

Beef with Cucumber and Celery Soup

1 pound shin, flank or stewing beef	¼ pound cucumber
	¼ pound celery
4 cups water	1 teaspoon salt
2 cups Broth	Pepper to taste

Repeat the preceding recipe using shin, flank or ordinary stewing beef, instead of spareribs. Simmer in water for 20 minutes. Skim and pour away one quarter of the water. Simmer very gently for 1 hour. Add Broth, cucumber and celery (1 cup of each cut into strips), season, and simmer together for another 30 minutes.

Sliced Beef with Watercress Soup

¼ pound beefsteak (rump or fillet)	3 cups Broth
	1 teaspoon salt
2 teaspoons cornstarch	Pepper to taste
1 bunch watercress	

Slice beef with sharp knife into 1-by-½-inch paper-thin slices.

Rub with cornstarch and half the salt. Clean watercress thoroughly, eliminate the muddier roots.

Heat Broth in a saucepan. Soon after boiling add beef and watercress to simmer in the Broth for 4 to 5 minutes. Adjust for seasonings and serve.

Sliced Beef with Tomato and Egg-flower Soup

¼ pound beef steak (rump or fillet)	3 medium-size tomatoes, sliced
1 teaspoon salt	1 egg
2 teaspoons cornstarch	Pepper to taste
3½ cups Broth	½ tablespoon soy sauce

Slice beef into 1-by-½-inch paper-thin slices. Rub with salt and cornstarch. Heat Broth in a saucepan. Soon after boiling add tomatoes to simmer for 3 minutes. Add beef and simmer for a further 3 minutes. Beat egg for 10 seconds and stream it along the prongs of a fork slowly into the soup. Add soy sauce, adjust for seasonings and serve.

Beef and Onion Soup

¾ pound stewing beef	2 tablespoons soy sauce
3 large onions	Pepper to taste
3 cups water	2 tablespoons sherry, optional
3 cups Broth	

Cut beef into 1-inch cubes. Slice onions into thin slices.

Boil beef in water for 30 minutes. Skim for impurities and pour away one-third of water. Add onion, Broth and soy sauce. Simmer together for 1 hour. Adjust for seasonings. Add sherry, simmer for a further minute and serve.

Sliced Pork and Mushroom Soup

¼ pound lean pork	3½ cups Broth
1 teaspoon salt	1 tablespoon sherry
2 teaspoons cornstarch	1 tablespoon soy sauce
¼ pound button mushrooms	Pepper to taste

Slice pork into thin 1-by-½-inch slices. Rub with half the salt and cornstarch. Slice mushrooms vertically into thin slices. Heat Broth in saucepan. When it starts to boil add pork. Simmer for 5 minutes. Add mushrooms and simmer for another 3 minutes. Add remaining salt and cornstarch, soy sauce and sherry, and adjust for seasoning. Stir and simmer for another 2 minutes and serve.

Sliced Pork and Celery Cabbage Soup

Repeat the preceding recipe, using ½ pound celery cabbage. Shred the cabbage and heat with pork from the beginning. If celery cabbage is not obtainable, use savoy cabbage (shredded) or celery.

Sliced Pork and Bean Sprout Soup

If bean sprouts are available they can be made into a soup with sliced pork as in Sliced Pork and Mushroom Soup, except that the sprouts will require no more than 2 minutes' simmering.

Sliced Pork and Broccoli Soup

Cut away the root and coarser parts of ¾ pound broccoli. Slice into individual branches. Boil for 3 minutes. Pour away water. Add broccoli to simmering Broth with pork, repeating recipe for Sliced Pork and Mushroom Soup.

Triple-shred Soup

1 breast of chicken	2 teaspoons cornstarch
3 tablespoons shredded ham	3½ cups Broth
3 tablespoons shredded abalone	2 tablespoons sherry
1 teaspoon salt	Pepper to taste

Slice chicken into thin strips. Rub chicken, ham and abalone with salt and cornstarch.

Bring Broth to boil in a saucepan. Add chicken, ham, abalone. Simmer gently for 3 minutes. Add sherry and adjust for seasonings. Stir and serve.

Lamb and Leek Soup

¼ pound lamb
½ teaspoon salt
2 teaspoons cornstarch
3 stalks young leek
1½ cups water

3 cups Broth
1½ tablespoons soy sauce
1 tablespoon dry sherry
Pepper to taste

Slice lamb into 1-by-½-inch very thin slices. Rub with salt and cornstarch. Cut leek into inch-length pieces.

Bring the water to boil in a saucepan. Add the leeks and simmer for 3 minutes. Pour away half the water. Pour in the Broth. Bring to boil, add the lamb, salt, and let simmer together for 5 minutes. Add soy sauce and sherry. Simmer for another minute. Adjust for seasonings and serve.

Green and White Soup

1 can green pea soup
1 cup Broth
1 teaspoon salt
2 tablespoons cornstarch,
   blended in 4 tablespoons
   water

1 cup Fu Yung Sauce
½ cup milk
Pepper to taste

Heat pea soup in a saucepan. Add half the Broth and half the salt, and thicken with half the cornstarch.

Heat remaining Broth, Fu Yung Sauce and milk in a second saucepan. Add remaining salt, and pepper, and thicken with remaining cornstarch.

When the contents of both saucepans are piping hot, stir and pour the green soup into a wide open soup bowl or tureen. Pour the white soup into the middle of the green soup. They can be poured and served in individual soup dishes in the same manner if so desired. The contrasting colors and alternating tastes make for an interesting presentation.

White Fish and Spring Green Soup

½ pound white fish fillet (sole, halibut, haddock, cod, bass, bream, etc.)
1½ teaspoons salt
1 egg white
1½ tablespoons cornstarch
½ pound spring greens (let-tuce, asparagus, broccoli or leeks)
2 cups water
3½ cups Broth
2 tablespoons chopped ham
1 teaspoon lemon juice
2 tablespoons dry sherry

Cut fish into slices 1½ inches by ½ inch. Rub with ½ tea-spoon salt. Beat egg white for half a minute; add cornstarch and beat together into a batter. Turn fish pieces in batter, covering them thoroughly. Chop greens into 1-inch squares; discard coarser leaves.

Boil the spring greens in water for 5 minutes. Pour away the water. Add the Broth and remaining salt. When the contents start to boil drop in the pieces of fish one by one. Simmer for 3 to 4 minutes. Sprinkle with chopped ham, lemon juice and sherry. Adjust for seasonings and serve as soon as the soup reboils.

White Fish and Green Pea Soup

½ pound fillet of white fish
  (sole, halibut, haddock,
  mullet, bream, bass, etc.)
1 egg white
1 tablespoon cornstarch

1 teaspoon salt
2 cans pea soup
1 cup Broth
2 teaspoons fresh lemon juice
2 tablespoons dry sherry

Cut fish into slices 1½ inches by ½ inch, and remove long bones. Beat egg white for half a minute, add cornstarch and beat together into a batter. Rub the pieces of fish with salt; turn and cover thoroughly with batter.

Heat pea soup in a saucepan. Add Broth. Stir and blend well. When soup starts to boil drop in the pieces of fish one by one. Allow the contents to simmer for 3 minutes. Sprinkle soup with lemon juice and sherry and serve.

Cream of Fish Soup with Shrimps

1 cup white fish fillet
2 cups Broth
2 teaspoons finely chopped
  lemon-rind shavings
1 cup Fu Yung Sauce
1 cup milk
1 teaspoon salt
½ cup shrimps, peeled

1½ tablespoons cornstarch,
  blended in 3 tablespoons
  water
1 teaspoon lemon juice
2 tablespoons sherry
3 tablespoons chopped ham
3 tablespoons chopped
  watercress

Boil fish for 5 minutes and mince into a paste. Heat Broth in a saucepan with chopped lemon peel for 2 minutes. Add Fu

Yung Sauce, milk and salt. When the contents start to boil add the minced fish and shrimps. Stir until contents are well blended. When it reboils thicken with cornstarch. Add lemon juice, sherry, half the chopped ham, half the chopped watercress. Stir. Allow the contents to simmer for half a minute. Adjust for seasoning. Pour into a large soup bowl or tureen and serve sprinkled with the remaining chopped ham and watercress.

Hot and Sour Soup
(*for five to six persons*)

½ cup lean pork, sliced into thin strips

4 tablespoons dried mushrooms, soaked and sliced into thin strips

3 tablespoons bamboo shoots, sliced into thin strips

3 tablespoons diced ham (¼-inch squares)

2 cups boiling water

3 cups Broth

3 tablespoons shrimps

3 tablespoons diced fish fillet (¼-inch squares)

2 tablespoons soy sauce

2 tablespoons wine vinegar

½ teaspoon salt

¼ teaspoon freshly milled black pepper, or to taste

2½ tablespoons cornstarch, blended with 4 tablespoons water

1 egg

Add pork, mushrooms, bamboo shoots and ham to the boiling water. Heat for 3 minutes. Skim for impurities and continue to simmer for half an hour. Add Broth, shrimps, fish and soy sauce, and continue to simmer for 10 minutes. Add vinegar, salt and pepper; thicken with cornstarch.

Beat egg in a cup for 10 seconds. Stream it in a thin stream into the soup along the prongs of a fork. Allow the egg a few seconds to set and harden. Stir and serve.

Extra Quick and Easy Soups

Chinese Chicken Noodle Soup

Chinese chicken noodle soups are served on festive occasions in China. Each guest is given a bowl as soon as he or she arrives, much as guests are given a glass of sherry or a cocktail when they arrive on such occasions in the West.

1 small packet egg noodles (or vermicelli)	2 tablespoons dry sherry
3½ cups Broth	3 to 4 tablespoons shredded cooked chicken
1 teaspoon salt	3 to 4 tablespoons shredded cooked ham
2 tablespoons soy sauce	

Drop noodles in a pan of boiling water to simmer for 5 minutes. Heat up the Broth in a separate saucepan. Loosen the noodles, drain and divide into 4 or 5 bowls. Sprinkle with salt, soy sauce and sherry. Pour boiling Broth into each of the bowls. Garnish the contents of each bowl with shredded chicken and ham.

Green Jade Soup

3½ cups Broth
  1 package creamed or
    minced frozen spinach
  1 teaspoon salt
  1 tablespoon soy sauce

1 tablespoon dry sherry
2 tablespoons cornstarch,
  blended in 3 tablespoons
  water

Heat Broth in a saucepan. Add spinach, allowing it to melt and dissolve slowly. When it has dissolved stir the soup. Add salt, soy sauce, sherry and cornstarch to thicken. Stir and serve.

Vegetable Soup

 4 cups Broth
½ teaspoon salt
Pepper to taste
  1 tablespoon soy sauce
  4 to 5 tablespoons bean sprouts
  4 to 5 tablespoons chopped
    spinach

1 tablespoon chopped chives
4 to 5 tablespoons sliced
  cucumber
4 to 5 tablespoons chopped
  watercress
2 tomatoes, each cut into 4
  pieces

Heat Broth in saucepan. Add seasonings and all the vegetables. Heat to boiling, simmer for 3 to 4 minutes and serve.

Shrimps and Peas in White Soup

1½ cups Broth
  1 cup Fu Yung Sauce
  1 cup milk
  2 tablespoons cornstarch,
    blended in 4 tablespoons
    water

1¼ teaspoons salt
  4 tablespoons frozen green
    peas
  4 tablespoons fresh shrimps,
    peeled
  1 tablespoon dry sherry

Heat Broth, Fu Yung Sauce and milk in a saucepan until the contents begin to boil. Thicken with cornstarch and add salt, peas, shrimps and sherry. On reboil simmer for half a minute and serve.

Egg-flower Soup (Soup of the Gods)

2½ pints Broth
  ½ cup water
Salt and pepper to taste

1½ tablespoons soy sauce
  1 tablespoon chopped chives
  1 egg

Heat Broth and water in a saucepan. Add salt and pepper to taste. Divide soy sauce and chopped chives, placing in four bowls. Beat egg in a cup or bowl for 15 seconds, stream it slowly in a small stream along the prongs of a fork into the Broth in the saucepan. Allow the egg 10 seconds to set. Stir, then pour the soup into the four bowls.

6

Rice Dishes

SINCE RICE AND PASTAS are two of the basic foods of China we shall deal with them before we deal with the great varieties of meat, fish and other savory dishes.

Boiled Rice

The cooking of very few dishes is as controversial as that of Boiled Rice. Many methods have been advanced, some complicated; others recommend the use of a Japanese thermostatic-controlled rice cooker. To the average Chinese cook all this appears unnecessary fuss, since the cooking of Boiled Rice is so simple. The following method is one of the simplest practicable in a modern kitchen.

1½ cups long-grain rice   1 cup boiling water
1½ cups water

After rinsing and washing the rice under running water for 10 seconds, drain, place in a saucepan and add 1½ cups water. Bring contents to boil for 1 minute. Lower the heat to a minimum, allowing the rice to simmer gently for 7 to 8 minutes, when the rice should have absorbed all the water in the pan, and appear quite dry. Pour in 1 cup boiling water. Replace the lid firmly. Allow the rice to simmer for a further 6 minutes. Turn the heat off altogether; now allow the rice to cook in its own heat for the next 4 to 5 minutes (do not open the lid during this time). The rice should then be ready to serve.

Fried Rice

Fried Rice is popular in the West, I think, partly because it is a self-contained dish which is simple and convenient to serve, and partly because in Chinese restaurants there are a great many bits and pieces of foods which can be conveniently cooked into the Fried Rice to advantage.

Vegetable Fried Rice

Vegetable Fried Rice is one of the simplest forms of Fried Rice, and it can be the basis from which other fancier forms can be prepared. Fried Rice is generally made from cold cooked rice, but I have found that it can be equally well prepared from hot cooked rice, so long as it is dry and flaky, and not sticky and messy (which it should not be).

4 eggs	1 tablespoon butter
1 teaspoon salt	2 tablespoons Broth
4 tablespoons vegetable oil	1 tablespoon soy sauce
2 tablespoons chopped onion	2 cups cooked rice
4 tablespoons green peas	
4 tablespoons button mush-	
rooms	

Beat eggs in a bowl for 10 seconds. Add half the salt. Heat oil in a large saucepan. When hot add onion and stir-fry for a minute. Pour in the beaten eggs. Tilt the pan so that the eggs will flow and cover the whole bottom of the pan. Lower the heat to very moderate. Heat the peas, mushrooms with butter, Broth and soy sauce in a small saucepan over high heat for about a minute.

Meanwhile, scramble the eggs and onion in the large saucepan. Add rice, sprinkle with remaining salt. Turn and scramble the rice thoroughly with the egg, oil and onion. Pour in in the peas and mushrooms from the small saucepan. Continue to turn, stir and scramble until all the rice is very hot. Do the turning, stirring, scrambling lightly without "messing up" the rice. It is important that Fried Rice should be served very hot.

This is best achieved not by turning up the heat, but by cooking over moderate heat for an extra couple of minutes.

Meat Fried Rice

Almost any type of meat can be used for frying with rice. The way to do it is to repeat the preceding recipe Vegetable Fried Rice and to use 4 to 5 tablespoons of meat diced into cubes about ¼ inch square. Fry the meat in 1 tablespoon oil in the small saucepan for a short while (chicken and beef for half a minute, veal and lamb for 1½ minutes, pork for 3 minutes) before adding mushrooms, peas and other ingredients. After the meat has been cooked with peas and mushrooms for 1 minute over high fire, add them to the rice for a final period of stir-frying. It is important to fry these additional materials separately before assembling them together in the final frying with the rice, if one is to avoid producing a messed-up dish. The meat will provide additional texture to the dish, apart from flavor.

Seafood Fried Rice

The majority of seafoods — such as shrimps, prawns, scallops, crab, abalone — can also be fried with rice. Cook the seafood in the same way as meat is cooked in the previous recipe, and then add it together with other ingredients into the Vegetable Fried Rice, for a final period of stir-frying. Seafoods do not generally require more than about a minute of frying before they can be added to the rice. They can, therefore, often be cooked in the small saucepan along with the peas and button mushrooms after the initial frying of those vegetables.

It should be remembered that the Chinese concept of Fried Rice is a dry dish. It is never slopping with gravy. It is best consumed along with a bowl of soup, which is taken in alternate spoonfuls with the rice.

Topped Rice

Topped rice is getting to be a popular dish because of its convenience — it being a self-contained dish. It can be eaten from a large plate while sitting in the living room or watching television. It also saves the cook or housewife from having to make a series of dishes for a proper sit-down dinner.

Almost any mixed stir-fried dish with gravy (especially those which have been briefly braised after frying) is suitable for "topping" rice. But if a pure meat dish is used it will be useful to have a pure vegetable dish to complement it. Say, for instance, we are to use a casserole of Red-cooked Beef or Red-cooked Pork, which are often better when warmed up from cold. Plain Fried Spinach or Quick-fried Cauliflower in Fu Yung Sauce will be good dishes to complement them. When warming up meat dishes, it is often the practice to add a small amount of soy sauce and sherry, which have the effect of rapidly livening them up.

Although any of the meat dishes described in this book —

such as Quick-fried Ribbons of Beef with Onion, Sweet and Sour Pork and Diced Chicken with Frozen Peas — will serve very well for topping rice, as will many of the seafood dishes, a few examples are provided below.

Portions: These recipes are for *two* persons, and Boiled Rice is presumed ready to hand.

Topped Rice with Sliced Soy Steak and Broccoli

1 pound beefsteak	6 tablespoons Broth
4 tablespoons Gunpowder Sauce	2 tablespoons vegetable oil
	3 cups hot Boiled Rice
1 small broccoli (1 cup when chopped)	

Slice steak into 1½-by-½-inch thin slices. Turn them in Gunpowder Sauce and leave to soak a few minutes.

Discard the coarser parts of the broccoli. Chop it into pieces or break into individual branches. Parboil broccoli for 4 to 5 minutes and drain, then place it in a saucepan, add Broth and leave over moderate heat for 3 to 4 minutes.

Heat oil in a frying pan. Add the sliced steak and stir-fry quickly over high heat for 1¼ minutes, reserving any left-over marinade (Gunpowder Sauce). Divide the hot Boiled Rice and spread out on two well-heated plates. Arrange the sliced steaks on one side of the rice. Replace the frying pan over heat; pour in the broccoli and liquid from the saucepan and the remaining marinade. Stir-fry over high heat for ¼ minute, divide and pour the vegetable and gravy over the

other side of the rice. To be eaten with spoon and fork —
served in this manner the food cannot be eaten with chopsticks, which require bowls.

Topped Rice with Diced Chicken, Mushrooms and Frozen Peas

1 breast of chicken	½ cup button mushrooms
1½ tablespoons cornstarch, blended in 3 tablespoons water	1 teaspoon salt
	4 tablespoons Fu Yung Sauce
½ cup Broth	2 tablespoons sherry
1 package frozen peas	3 cups hot Boiled Rice

Dice chicken into ¼-inch cubes. Add half cornstarch mixture and mix well.

Heat Broth in a saucepan. Add peas and mushrooms. Bring
to boil and simmer over moderate heat for 3 minutes. Turn
heat high and add the chicken and salt. Stir for 20 seconds and
pour in remaining cornstarch, Fu Yung Sauce and sherry.
Stir for another 20 seconds.

Divide and spread the rice onto two well-heated serving
plates. Ladle out the chicken, peas, mushrooms and gravy
over the rice. Serve piping hot.

Topped Rice with Sweet and Sour Pork and Fu Yung Cauliflower

3 cups hot Boiled Rice   Quick-fried Cauliflower in
Sweet and Sour Pork   Fu Yung Sauce

Although the recipes for Sweet and Sour Pork and Quick-fried Cauliflower in Fu Yung Sauce were intended for three or four persons, they were meant to be eaten with two or three other dishes. The quantities in the two recipes are consequently just right for two portions if eaten with rice as a complete meal. The hot rice should be spread out on the plates, and the pork and cauliflower with their contrasting sauces should be placed and poured separately and neatly over the rice.

7

Pasta or Noodle Dishes

THERE ARE MANY TYPES of noodle dishes in China. The best-known of the Chinese noodles in the West is, of course, Chow Mein, which means Fried Noodles. There are also Soup Noodles, Gravy Noodles and Tossed Noodles. Soup Noodles, served in China, is not very suitable for Western consumption as it is usually contained in a large bowl with so many noodles in it that a bowl will fill you up for a meal and you would not be able to eat much of anything else! In China Soup Noodles is taken for a snack meal, with nothing else to go with it. The other types of Chinese noodle dishes should be useful for providing a Western snack meal, or even as a supplementary dish to the other dishes in a proper multidish dinner.

Chow Mein (Fried Noodles)

Chow Mein is different from Italian spaghettis, mainly in that the pasta is given a topping of meats and vegetables only after the noodles have been fried in oil and meat gravy. Otherwise they are very similar (some say that Italian pastas were originally brought over from China by Marco Polo), and spaghettis and egg noodles or vermicelli can all be used for the purpose. As a rule Chinese noodles and egg noodles or vermicelli only require 6 to 8 minutes' boiling before they can be drained and made use of; spaghettis generally require 15 to 16 minutes' boiling, before they are sufficiently soft for use.

As with Fried Rice almost any stir-fried meat and vegetable dishes can be used to top the Fried Noodles. The following few recipes should provide instances of how these noodle dishes are cooked and set out.

Portions: All the recipes in this chapter are meant for two or three people.

Beef and Onion Chow Mein with Watercress

½ pound noodles
⅔ pound beefsteak
1½ teaspoons sugar
2 tablespoons soy sauce
Pepper to taste
3 tablespoons vegetable oil
2 large onions, thinly sliced

1 tablespoon butter
4 tablespoons Meat Gravy
Sauce
2 tablespoons dry sherry
3 tablespoons chopped
watercress

Parboil the noodles for 6 to 8 minutes. Drain, rinse under

running water and put aside. Shred beef into thin strips, add sugar, soy sauce and pepper to marinate for a few minutes.

Heat 2 tablespoons oil in a frying pan. Add onion to stir-fry over high heat for 2 minutes. Add the marinated beef and continue to stir-fry for 1 minute. Remove from pan and put aside.

Add the remaining oil, butter and Meat Gravy Sauce to the same pan. Place over high heat. Pour in the parboiled noodles. Turn and stir-fry slowly for 1 minute. Turn down the heat to low, and continue to stir-fry slowly for another 2 minutes. Divide the noodles, placing on two well-heated serving plates or bowls. Return the frying pan to the heat. Return the beef and onion to the pan. Add sherry. Stir-fry for ½ minute over high heat and top the two plates or bowls of noodles with the onion and beef and sprinkle with chopped watercress.

Chicken and Mushroom Chow Mein with Green Beans or Pea Pods

½ pound noodles
3 large mushrooms
3 tablespoons vegetable oil
1 chopped onion
½ cup shredded green beans
   or pea pods
1 cup shredded cooked
   chicken meat

½ teaspoon salt
1 tablespoon soy sauce
1 tablespoon butter
3 tablespoons Meat Gravy
   Sauce
2 tablespoons dry sherry

Parboil noodles for 6 to 8 minutes. Drain, rinse under cold

running water and put aside. Shred mushrooms and clean thoroughly under running water.

Heat 2 tablespoons oil in a large frying pan. When hot add onion and green beans and stir-fry for 1½ minutes. Add mushrooms and chicken. Sprinkle with salt and ½ tablespoon soy sauce. Stir-fry gently for another 1½ minutes over moderate heat. Remove all the contents from the pan with perforated spoon and put aside.

Return the pan to the heat. Add remaining oil, butter and Meat Gravy Sauce. Heat and stir together over moderate heat for half a minute, when the oil, butter and gravy should become well mixed. Pour in the boiled and drained noodles. Turn and stir-fry it slowly in the pan for 1 minute. Lower the heat, and continue to stir-fry slowly for another 2 minutes, when the noodles should be heated through. Divide the noodles and place on two serving plates. Return the frying pan over the heat. Add sherry and remaining soy sauce. Return the chicken, mushroom and beans to the pan for half a minute of stir-frying over high heat. Divide the contents and top the two platefuls of noodles with them.

Chicken and Shrimp Chow Mein with French Beans or Pea Pods

Repeat the preceding recipe substituting ½ cup shrimp meat for mushrooms.

Lamb and Leek Chow Mein

½ pound noodles
½ pound lamb (from leg)
2 tablespoons soy sauce
1 teaspoon sugar
Paprika to taste
3 tablespoons vegetable oil
1 clove garlic, crushed

3 to 4 stalks young leek, cut
   into 1-inch segments
4 tablespoons Meat Gravy
   Sauce
2 tablespoons sherry
1 tablespoon butter

Parboil noodles 6 to 8 minutes. Drain, rinse under running water, put aside.

Shred lamb. Add soy sauce, sugar and paprika to marinate for a few minutes.

Heat 2 tablespoons oil in a frying pan. Add garlic and leek to stir-fry together over high heat for 1½ minutes. Add the marinated lamb, and stir-fry together for another 2 minutes. Remove and put aside.

Add remainder of oil and Meat Gravy Sauce to the frying pan. Stir and heat over moderate heat. Pour in the parboiled noodles. Turn and stir-fry slowly for 1 minute. Reduce the heat to low and continue to stir-fry slowly for 2 minutes. Divide the noodles and set on two well-heated plates.

Add sherry and butter to the frying pan. Reheat the lamb and leek in it over high heat. Stir-fry for ½ minute. Divide the lamb mixture in two and top the noodles.

Pork and Bean Sprout Chow Mein

½ pound noodles
½ pound lean pork
1½ tablespoons soy sauce
1½ teaspoons sugar
Pepper to taste
3 tablespoons vegetable oil
1 tablespoon butter

4 tablespoons Meat Gravy
Sauce
2 cups bean sprouts
½ teaspoon salt
4 tablespoons Broth
2 tablespoons sherry

Parboil noodles as in preceding recipe.

Shred pork. Add soy sauce, sugar and pepper to marinate for a few minutes.

Heat 2 tablespoons oil in a frying pan. Add pork and stir-fry over high heat for 2 minutes. Lower heat to moderate, and continue to stir-fry for 2 minutes. Remove pork and put aside.

Add butter and Meat Gravy Sauce to the frying pan over high heat. Stir and pour in the noodles. Turn and stir-fry for 1 minute. Lower heat to very moderate, and continue to stir-fry slowly for 2 minutes. Divide the noodles and set into two well-heated plates.

Add remaining oil to the frying pan. Turn the heat high. Add the bean sprouts. Sprinkle with salt and stir-fry for ½ minute. Add Broth, continue to stir-fry for ½ minute. Add the pork and sherry and continue to stir-fry over high heat for 1 minute. Divide the pork and bean sprouts into two parts and top the noodles with them.

Chow Mein with Shredded Duck and Celery

½ pound noodles
3 stalks celery
3 tablespoons vegetable oil
1 teaspoon sugar
1½ tablespoons soy sauce
 1 cup shredded roast duck
  meat

1 teaspoon Tabasco
2 tablespoons dry sherry
1 tablespoon butter
4 tablespoons Meat Gravy
 Sauce
2 tablespoons chopped
 parsley

Prepare noodles as in preceding recipes. Cut and shred celery
into thin strips.

Heat 2 tablespoons oil in a frying pan. Add celery and stir-
fry over high heat for 1 minute. Add sugar and soy sauce and
continue to stir-fry for a half minute. Add duck meat,
Tabasco and 1 tablespoon sherry and stir-fry together for a
further half minute. Remove and put aside.

Add remainder of oil, butter and Meat Gravy Sauce into the
frying pan, over high heat. Pour in the noodles. Turn and
stir-fry for 1 minute. Reduce heat to low and continue to
stir-fry slowly for a further 2 minutes. Arrange the noodles
on two well-heated serving plates. Add remaining sherry and
chopped parsley to the frying pan over high heat. Return the
duck and celery to the pan. Stir-fry for ½ minute. Divide
the duck and celery into two parts and top the noodles with
them.

Gravy Noodles

Gravy Noodles takes longer to prepare than Chow Mein, as it must be served with large chunks of meat which have been lengthily cooked. But if the meats are ready it can take a shorter time to prepare than Chow Mein. Here, in the recipes to follow, we presume the meat is ready. Serve these dishes with chopsticks; eat by lifting the bowl to the mouth and resting the elbow on the table, as we do in China.

Gravy Noodles with Red-cooked Pork and Spinach

½ pound noodles
1½ cups Red-cooked Pork
¾ cup Meat Gravy Sauce
1½ tablespoons cornstarch, blended in 3 tablespoons cold Broth
2 tablespoons vegetable oil

1 clove garlic, crushed
1 tablespoon chopped onion
3 cups chopped spinach
2 tablespoons Gunpowder Sauce
2 tablespoons sherry

Prepare the noodles as in the preceding recipes.

Heat pork in half the Meat Gravy Sauce in a small saucepan. Pour the remainder of the sauce into a larger saucepan, heat and thicken together with cornstarch mixture. When hot, add the noodles and turn them into the thickened sauce. Heat over low heat for 3 minutes. Pour into two large bowls.

Heat oil in a frying pan. When hot add garlic and onion.

Stir-fry for ½ minute. Add spinach, Gunpowder Sauce and sherry. Stir-fry over high heat for 2 minutes.

Meanwhile, divide pork and spinach sauce into two parts. Pour and add them to the two bowls of noodles, decorating them on top with the spinach. Then pour the hot gravy from the frying pan into the bowls.

Gravy Noodles with Spiced Beef and Tomatoes

½ pound noodles
3 tomatoes
½ pound Red-cooked Beef
¾ cup Meat Gravy Sauce
1½ tablespoons cornstarch, blended in 3 tablespoons cold Broth

1 cup Broth
2 tablespoons dry sherry
2 teaspoons chopped chives
1 tablespoon vegetable oil
1 tablespoon Gunpowder Sauce

Prepare the noodles as in the preceding recipes. Cut each tomato into four.

Heat beef in half the Meat Gravy Sauce in a small saucepan. Pour the remainder of sauce into a large saucepan. Add Broth. Set over moderate heat. When hot add cornstarch to thicken.

Add the noodles. Turn them in the thickened gravy for 3 minutes over low heat. Divide, place in two bowls. Add sherry to beef, turn up heat.

Divide the beef and pour it, together with gravy, on top of the noodles in the two bowls. Fry the tomatoes and chives quickly in oil and Gunpowder Sauce. Add to the foods in the bowls to decorate.

Gravy Noodles with Chicken and Oyster

½ pound noodles
1 breast of chicken
1½ tablespoons vegetable oil
1 teaspoon finely chopped lemon-peel shavings
1 teaspoon salt
1 cup Broth
½ cup oysters (1 dozen fresh, shelled)
2 tablespoons sherry

1 tablespoon butter
½ cup Fu Yung Sauce
1 tablespoon cornstarch, blended in 2 tablespoons cold Broth
½ cup button mushrooms
2 tablespoons chopped parsley
2 tablespoons chopped ham

Prepare noodles as in preceding recipes. Dice chicken into ¼-inch cubes.

Heat oil in saucepan. When hot add chicken and chopped lemon peel. Stir-fry for ½ minute. Add salt, and half the Broth. When the mixture starts to boil put in the oysters. Turn and set at moderate heat for 1½ minutes. Pour in the sherry. Heat gently for another minute.

Meanwhile, heat the remaining Broth in another saucepan, together with butter and Fu Yung Sauce, adding cornstarch to thicken. Adjust for seasonings. Pour in the noodles and turn them in the thickened sauce for 3 minutes over moderate heat. Divide the noodles, placing in two bowls. Pour the chicken, oysters and mushrooms over noodles. Sprinkle with chopped parsley and ham.

Gravy Noodles with Crabmeat

½ pound noodles	1 cup Broth
2 stalks young leek	2 tablespoons sherry
2 tablespoons vegetable oil	½ cup Meat Gravy Sauce
2 tablespoons chopped onion	1 tablespoon cornstarch,
1 clove garlic, crushed	blended in 2 tablespoons
¼ pound (1 cup) crabmeat,	cold Broth
fresh, cooked or canned	1 tablespoon chopped chives
½ teaspoon salt	

Parboil and prepare noodles as in the preceding recipes. Cut leeks into 1-inch segments.

Heat oil in a saucepan. Add onion and garlic, stir-fry over high heat for half a minute. Add leeks and continue to stir-fry for 1 minute. Add crabmeat and salt. Stir-fry together for 1 minute. Pour in 4 tablespoons Broth and sherry. Stir and heat for a further half minute.

Meanwhile, add the remaining Broth to the Meat Gravy Sauce in a large saucepan. Heat over moderate flame and thicken with cornstarch mixture. Add the noodles. Turn them in the gravy over moderate heat for 2 minutes. Sprinkle noodles with chives, and add one quarter of the crabmeat mixture. Turn it with the noodles. Adjust the seasonings and divide the noodles, placing them in two large bowls. Top the contents of the two bowls with the remainder of the crabmeat and leeks.

Topped and Scrambled Noodles

This particular style of noodles is very similar to the Italian Spaghetti Boulognaise or Milanaise, where the prepared sauce is mixed into the noodles by the diners themselves, except with the Chinese noodles the sauce used is slightly more piquant than the Italian, and shredded vegetables with crunchy texture are always served to provide a contrast of texture with the softness of the noodles. This adds a new dimension to the dishes which are, in fact, pasta with shredded vegetable salad.

Topped and Scrambled Noodles with Shredded Duck and Mustard Sauce

2 to 3 teaspoons dry mustard
2 teaspoons cornstarch,
  blended in 2 tablespoons
  Broth
6 tablespoons Meat Gravy
  Sauce

1 tablespoon butter
1½ tablespoons vegetable oil
½ pound noodles
1 tablespoon chopped chives
1½ cups shredded roast duck
  meat

For accompaniment:

1 saucerful shredded
  cucumber
1 saucerful shredded radish
1 small bowlful bean sprouts

1 saucedish mixed pickles
1 saucedish chutneys
1 saucedish vinegar

Blend mustard with 1 tablespoon water. Blend again with blended cornstarch. Heat Meat Gravy Sauce and butter in small saucepan. When hot add the mustard mixture and stir over low heat until it thickens. Add oil and stir thoroughly. Pour sauce into serving bowl.

Meanwhile prepare noodles as in preceding recipes, putting into two bowls while still very hot. Sprinkle immediately with chives. Scatter the shredded duck meat over them. Ladle a couple of tablespoonfuls or more of the mustard sauce over the duck and noodles. Toss and scramble them together, and eat in conjunction with all the attendant shredded vegetables, pickles, chutneys.

Topped and Scrambled Noodles with Shredded Chicken and Ham and Parsley Dressing

½ pound noodles
1 tablespoon chopped chives
6 tablespoons Broth
2 tablespoons chopped parsley
½ teaspoon salt

2 tablespoons vegetable oil
1 cup shredded roast chicken
4 tablespoons shredded cooked ham

Prepare the noodles as in the preceding recipes, putting into two bowls while still hot. Sprinkle immediately with chopped chives.

Heat Broth in a small saucepan. As soon as it boils add parsley and salt, and remove from heat. Pour in the oil, stir and beat for about ½ minute. Pour this "dressing" into a saucebowl.

Divide and arrange the shredded chicken and ham over the noodles. Ladle on the dressing. To be eaten hot or cold, with the same accompaniments as in the preceding recipe.

Topped and Scrambled Noodles with Piquant Meat Sauce

3½ tablespoons vegetable oil
  1 clove garlic, chopped
  ½ tablespoon chopped capers
  1 tablespoon finely chopped
    onion
  1 cup minced pork
  2 tablespoons soy sauce
    (heavy type if available)

  ½ teaspoon Tabasco
1½ teaspoons sugar
  4 tablespoons Broth
  ½ tablespoon cornstarch,
    blended in 2 tablespoons
    cold Broth
  ½ pound noodles

For accompaniment:

  1 small plateful bean sprouts
  1 saucerful shredded
    cucumber
  ½ saucerful spring onion,
    1-inch segments
  ½ saucerful shredded celeriac

  ½ saucerful shredded radish
  1 saucedish chutney
  1 saucedish mixed sweet
    pickles
  1 saucedish vinegar

Heat oil in a saucepan. Add garlic, capers and chopped onion, and stir-fry for ½ minute. Add pork. Mix and stir-fry for 2 minutes over high heat. Pour in the soy sauce, Tabasco and sugar and add Broth. Stir and leave to cook for 2 minutes after reducing heat to low. Add cornstarch mixture to thicken. Stir and cook for another half minute.

Meanwhile parboil the noodles as in the preceding recipes without rinsing under cold running water. Instead drain the noodles, and divide immediately, placing in two bowls while still very hot. Pour or ladle a suitable quantity of the prepared meat sauce over each bowl of noodles (quantity depends on taste). Add the various shredded vegetables and bean sprouts, which are placed on the table to mix with the noodles and meat sauce. Additional quantities of chutney and pickles can also be added if desired. The resultant noodles will have the quality of being meaty, crunchy, piquant and filling all at the same time. This type of noodles is the favorite of the peasantry in North China (who would use bean paste rather than soy bean sauce for preparing the meat sauce).

Topped and Scrambled Noodles with Beef-tomato Sauce

Repeat the preceding recipe, substituting minced beef for pork, and use only 1 tablespoon soy sauce, adding 3 tablespoons tomato purée and ½ teaspoon salt. All the attending shredded vegetables and the bean sprouts remain the same.

Topped and Scrambled Noodles with Vegetarian Dressings

½ pound noodles   1 tablespoon chopped chives

For Peanut Butter Dressing:

3 tablespoons peanut butter   2 tablespoons dry sherry
2 tablespoons vegetable oil   1 teaspoon Tabasco
2 tablespoons soy sauce

For Cucumber Dressing:

1 cup cucumber, sliced to thin
  strips
2 tablespoons vegetable oil
2 tablespoons vinegar

2 tablespoons soy sauce
3 teaspoons sugar
1 tablespoon sherry

Mix and blend the ingredients of the dressings separately and place the Peanut Butter Dressing in a saucebowl and the Cucumber Dressing in a soupbowl.

Prepare the noodles as in the preceding recipes and divide into two or three portions, placing in separate bowls. Sprinkle immediately with chopped chives.

Pour dressings over the noodles, and eat along with optional other shredded vegetables, pickles and chutneys.

8

Pork

PORK IS the most widely used meat in China. It is cooked both on its own and in combination with other food materials.

When cooked on its own, pork usually requires very little preparation but fairly lengthy cooking. The reverse is true when it is cooked in combination; for then the meat has to be reduced to the required size before it is cooked or stir-fried, together with vegetables or other materials which also have to be reduced to small sizes and shapes. In that case preparation usually consumes more time than cooking. However, on its own or in combination, there are points in the process which can be shortened or simplified. We shall deal here with both styles of cooking pork.

Red-cooked Pork

Pork is "red-cooked" when it is slowly cooked in ample gravy or sauce with one or two other ingredients; in our case we shall simply use Gunpowder Sauce, which is the standard combination of ingredients for this type of cooking. The general technique of *red-cooking* is to conduct the second or last stage of the cooking very slowly over very low heat and in very little liquid (not more than one-quarter to one-third the weight of the meat), in order that the taste and juices of the meat will not all be dispersed into the soup. As far as possible the meat should be cooked in its own juices, with the basic flavors and liquid of the ingredients penetrating into the meat, which prevents it from drying as well as helping to tenderize it during its comparatively long period of slow simmering. In the Western kitchen red-cooking can be practiced even more easily since the heat regulator is part and parcel of every modern cooker and oven.

Red-cooked Pork (*Basic*)

3 cups water
1 3-to-4-pound leg of pork
  with skin
2 tablespoons soy sauce

½ cup Gunpowder Sauce
2 teaspoons sugar
2 tablespoons sherry

Bring water to boil in a large saucepan. Add pork; boil for 10 minutes. Pour away two-thirds of the water, together with any impurities. Add soy sauce and simmer for 20 minutes, turning the pork over once and reducing the liquid to about half. Transfer the pork and liquid to a casserole with lid. Pour half the Gunpowder Sauce over the pork. Turn the pork over in the strengthened liquid a few times. Place the casserole in a preheated oven at 400 degrees. After half an hour, turn the pork over and add sugar, sherry and remaining Gunpowder Sauce. Reduce heat to 350 degrees. Cook for one more hour at this reduced heat, turning the meat over twice in that time.

After 2 hours' cooking the pork should be sufficiently tender to be taken to pieces with a pair of chopsticks on the table, or it can be sliced with a knife.

Portions: This dish should be served with at least two other dishes, one of which has to be vegetable; all to be eaten with rice. The amount here should be sufficient for four to eight persons.

Red-cooked Pork with Eggs

Repeat the preceding recipe. Simmer 4 or 5 hard-boiled eggs (shelled) in 1 cup soy sauce for 4 to 5 minutes and add to the Red-cooked Pork gravy during the last half-hour of cooking. Serve by surrounding the pork with the eggs, which have been sliced in half.

Red-cooked Pork with Spinach

Repeat basic recipe for Red-cooked Pork. Quick-fry ½ pound spinach (after cleaning and removing coarser bits) in

3 tablespoons vegetable oil and ½ teaspoon salt for 2 minutes over high heat, and insert it under the pork in the casserole during the last 15 minutes' cooking, adding 1 additional tablespoon each of sherry and Gunpowder Sauce.

Red-cooked Pork with Chestnuts

Repeat basic recipe for Red-cooked Pork. Boil 1 pound chestnut meat for 30 minutes (simultaneously as the pork is cooked), drain and add to the pork gravy during the last 30 minutes' cooking in the casserole. An additional tablespoon of Gunpowder Sauce and 2 tablespoons sherry should be added when the chestnuts are put into the casserole.

Chopped Red-cooked Pork

To save time in cooking, as well as to facilitate easier mixing with other materials, as often as not pork is cooked chopped into smaller pieces. Here in the following recipes they are either cut into 1½-inch squares, or 2-by-1-inch oblongs, preferably with skin attached to each piece, as in China we regard pork skin, when thoroughly cooked, as meat jelly — excellent for eating with rice.

Chopped Red-cooked Pork with Carrots

2 pounds pork (leg or shoulder)	1 pound carrots
2 tablespoons soy sauce	4 tablespoons Gunpowder Sauce
1 cup water	2 tablespoons sherry

Cut pork into 2-by-1-inch pieces, place in heavy saucepan, add soy sauce and bring to boil in 1 cup water. Simmer for half an hour. Clean and cut carrots into 1-inch-long triangular wedge-shaped pieces. Add carrots, Gunpowder Sauce and sherry. Simmer over very low fire for a further hour, turning the materials over a couple of times in the process.

Chopped Red-cooked Pork with Abalone

Repeat the preceding recipe. Slice abalone (½ can, discarding liquid) into thin slices and add to pork three minutes before serving. (Abalone hardens when overcooked.) Turn pork and abalone over a few times and serve.

Chopped Red-cooked Pork with Salted Fish (Haddock) and Anchovy

Repeat recipe for Red-cooked Pork with Carrots. Soak ½ pound salted fish in water for 1 hour before use. Cut into the same size pieces as the pork and add to the latter, together with 2 teaspoons anchovy during the last half hour of cooking.

Chopped Red-cooked Pork with Chestnuts

Repeat the recipe for Chopped Red-cooked Pork with Carrots. Boil 1 pound chestnut meat for 20 minutes and drain before adding to the pork for 1 hour's simmer together.

Chopped Red-cooked Pork with Potatoes

This dish can be eaten on its own with one vegetable dish, without rice.

Repeat recipe for Chopped Red-cooked Pork with Carrots, using 2 pounds potatoes instead of carrots, adding the potatoes, which have been peeled and parboiled for 3 minutes, during the last 30 minutes of cooking, along with ½ cup Broth, and using 6 tablespoons Gunpowder Sauce.

Red-cooked Spareribs

2 to 2½ pounds spareribs	2 tablespoons soy sauce
1 large onion	1 cup Broth
Pepper or paprika to taste	2½ tablespoons Gunpowder
½ tablespoon sugar	Sauce
2 tablespoons sherry	2 tablespoons vegetable oil

Boil spareribs in a panful of water for 10 minutes. Drain. Cut into individual ribs. Chop onion and add it to the ribs in a saucepan. Sprinkle with pepper or paprika, sugar, sherry and soy sauce, and add Broth. Simmer gently under cover for ½ hour, turning the ribs over 3 times; heat until the ribs are nearly dry. Brush or rub the ribs with Gunpowder Sauce and oil, and place in a roasting pan to be inserted in a preheated oven at 375 degrees for 15 minutes. To be eaten with fingers, as a starter.

White-cooked Pork

Pork is said to be "white-cooked" when it is boiled, simmered or steamed plain, without the use of soy sauce. When cooked in such a manner it is invariably eaten dipped in a number of sauces which are provided in small saucedishes placed at various convenient points on the table.

Portions: For four to nine persons, to be served with a couple of other dishes.

Chopped White-cooked Pork with Ham

2 pounds pork (leg or shoulder)
1 pound belly of pork (with skin)
1 pound bacon or ham

1 cup water
2 teaspoons sugar
1½ teaspoon salt
4 tablespoons sherry

Boil both types of pork and bacon or ham in ample water for 15 minutes. Drain and pour away water. Chop pork into 2-by-½-inch pieces. Place the meats, alternately interlaced, in a heavy saucepan. Add 1 cup water, sugar, salt and sherry. Simmer under cover over low heat for 1 hour. Serve in a bowl.

White-cooked Pork (*in whole piece*)

3 pounds pork (leg or shoulder)   1 tablespoon chopped lemon
8 cups water   rind
2 teaspoons salt

Place pork in water in saucepan. Bring to boil and add salt
and lemon rind. Simmer under cover for 1¼ hours. Drain,
reserving stock for other uses. When cold, slice pork into thin
slices, to be served in conjunction with the following dips:

   3 tablespoons soy sauce mixed with 2 teaspoons Tabasco
   3 tablespoons soy sauce mixed with 2 tablespoons vinegar
   3 tablespoons soy sauce mixed with 3 teaspoons mustard
   2 tablespoons soy sauce mixed with 2 tablespoons tomato
      sauce and 1 teaspoon Tabasco

Chopped White-cooked Pork with Abalone and Cabbage (*or Celery*)

Repeat the preceding recipe, substituting 1 can of abalone for
ham but adding the abalone only during the last 5 minutes of
cooking and adding cabbage (Chinese cabbage, savoy cabbage
or celery, cut into 2-inch pieces) during the last 30 minutes.
When serving in a deep-sided dish, place the meat and abalone
on top of the vegetable.

Roast and Braised Pork

Cha Shao Roast (or Barbecued) Pork

3 pounds fillet of pork
1 cup Gunpowder Sauce

1 tablespoon honey
3 tablespoons sherry

Cut pork (with grain) into pieces, approximately 6 by 2 inches, and 1 to 1½ inches thick. Soak them in Gunpowder Sauce to marinate for half an hour, turning the pieces over now and then.

When ready, drain (reserve marinade). Place the strips of pork on a metal rack over the roasting pan (filled with some water to prevent burning of drippings) and insert into an oven preheated to 400 degrees. Roast for 15 minutes. Add and stir honey and sherry into the remaining marinade. Turn the strips of pork in the marinade for a second dip. Turn them over in it a few more times and place on rack to roast in the oven for another 10 minutes at 375 degrees. Dip again in marinade and roast 10 minutes more at same temperature.

Serve by slicing the pork across the strip against the grain into ¼-inch-thick slices.

Braised Roast Pork Chops

2 to 3 pounds pork chops
½ cup Broth
4 tablespoons sherry

2 tablespoons soy sauce
2½ tablespoons Gunpowder Sauce

Braise or simmer pork chops in Broth, soy sauce and sherry for 25 minutes over moderate heat, turning the chops over every couple of minutes, until they are nearly dried. Pour the Gunpowder Sauce over the chops. Brush with a pastry brush until they are evenly covered. Place on a roasting pan, and insert in an oven preheated to 400 degrees for 10 minutes. Serve as ordinary pork chops. (Double cooking makes them very tender.)

Twice-cooked Pork

2 pounds pork (leg or shoulder)	½ teaspoon salt
3 tablespoons vegetable oil	1 tablespoon tomato purée
3 teaspoons chopped capers	½ cup chopped young leeks
2 cloves garlic, chopped	2 tablespoons sherry
2 teaspoons Tabasco	1½ tablespoons soy sauce

Boil pork in water for 30 minutes. Slice into thin 2-by-1½-inch pieces. Heat oil in a large frying pan. Add capers, garlic, Tabasco, salt, purée; stir-fry for half a minute. Add pork and stir-fry rapidly over high heat for 2½ minutes and remove. Add leeks to stir-fry in the remaining oil for 1½ minutes. Return the pork to the pan. Add sherry and soy sauce. Stir-fry together, still over high heat, for 1½ minutes and serve.

Sweet and Sour Pork

1½ pounds lean pork	4 tablespoons vegetable oil
½ teaspoon salt	1 green or red sweet pepper
½ tablespoon cornstarch	1 cup Sweet and Sour Sauce

Dice pork into ¾-inch cubes. Sprinkle and rub with salt and cornstarch.

Heat 3 tablespoons oil in a large frying pan. When very hot add pork and stir-fry over high heat for 7 to 8 minutes. Remove pan from heat and put aside.

Heat 1 tablespoon oil in another frying pan. Slice the sweet pepper into narrow 2-inch-long strips. Add them to the hot oil to quick-fry for half a minute. Lower heat and pour in the Sweet and Sour Sauce. Turn the pepper over in the sauce until the latter thickens. Pour in the pork from the other pan, stir-fry them together over high heat, stirring slowly for half a minute and serve.

Stir-fried Pork Dishes

The pork in the following recipes is either in thin slices or in shreds or minced; and being stir-fried it usually takes only a very short time to cook, but somewhat longer to prepare, as it is necessary first of all to reduce the meat to the correct size and shape. The vegetables, which are cooked in combination with the meat, are similarly reduced. All the stir-fried pork dishes are suitable for garnishing Chow Mein or Topped Rice.

In Chinese cooking, whether pork is sliced into thin slices or is shredded into matchstick strips before being cooked depends largely upon the shape and size of the other materials with which it is cooked, or with which it is intended to be served. For instance, when cooked with bean sprouts, or ribbons of onion, or served with noodles, the pork is invariably cut into strips or shreds; on the other hand, when the meat is intended to be cooked with flat slices of sweet pepper or cucumber or cabbage or mushrooms, the pork is generally cut into flat thin slices.

Portions: The following recipes are meant for three to four persons and to be eaten with rice, along with at least two other dishes. They are also suitable for seven to eight persons if the total number of dishes on the table is increased by two or three. If a person is dining alone he can use one of the dishes to top his rice or garnish his noodles, to the accompaniment of a soup, to make a complete meal.

Stir-fried Pork with Bean Sprouts

¾ pound lean pork
3 tablespoons vegetable oil
1 tablespoon soy sauce
1 teaspoon salt
Pepper to taste
1 clove garlic, crushed

2 stalks spring onion (in 1½-inch segments)
2 tablespoons sherry
1 teaspoon sugar
2 cups bean sprouts
3 tablespoons Broth

Slice pork against grain into shreds (approximately matchstick size).

Heat 2 tablespoons oil in a large frying pan. When hot add

pork and stir-fry over high heat for 3 minutes, adding soy sauce during the last minute of stir-frying. Remove and keep hot.

Add remaining oil to the pan. Add salt, pepper, garlic and spring onion, sherry and sugar. Stir-fry together over high heat for half a minute. Pour in the bean sprouts. Continue to stir-fry over high heat for 1½ minutes. Add Broth, return the pork to the pan, stir-fry together for 2 minutes and serve.

Stir-fried Shredded Pork with Spring Onions

¾ pound lean pork
3 tablespoons vegetable oil
1 clove garlic, crushed
½ teaspoon salt
1½ tablespoons soy sauce
6 stalks spring onion (1½-inch segments)

2 tablespoons sherry
½ tablespoon cornstarch, blended in 3 tablespoons cold Broth
Pepper to taste
1 teaspoon sugar

Slice pork into shredded strips (against grain).

Heat oil in a large frying pan. When hot add garlic, salt and pork, and stir-fry together over high heat for 2½ minutes. Add soy sauce and continue to stir-fry for 1 minute. Add spring onion, sherry, cornstarch mixture, pepper, sugar; stir-fry for a further 1½ minutes and serve.

Stir-fried Shredded Pork with Asparagus

Repeat the preceding recipe using asparagus instead of celery

(4 to 6 stalks of asparagus parboiled for 3 minutes with tough part removed, and each stalk shredded into thin strips). Increase the final stir-frying to 3½ minutes, adding 2 tablespoons additional Broth.

Stir-fried Shredded Pork with Celery

Repeat the preceding recipe, substituting twice the quantity of celery for spring onion, and lengthening the final stir-fry to 2½ minutes.

Stir-fried Shredded Pork with Peas and Mushrooms

¾ pound lean pork
1 small package frozen green
  . peas
4 to 6 large mushrooms
2 tablespoons vegetable oil
½ teaspoon salt
1 tablespoon butter

1½ teaspoons sugar
1 tablespoon soy sauce
2 tablespoons sherry
1 teaspoon Tabasco
½ tablespoon cornstarch,
  blended with 2 tablespoons
  Broth

Slice pork into strips. Thaw peas and slice mushrooms into shreds similar to the pork strips.

Heat oil in a frying pan. When hot, add pork, sprinkle with salt and stir-fry over high heat for 3 minutes. Remove and keep warm. Add butter to the pan, along with peas and mushrooms. Stir-fry together for 1 minute. Add sugar, soy sauce, sherry, Tabasco, and return the pork to the pan. Stir-fry all together for 1 minute. Add cornstarch mixture. Heat for a further ¾ minute. Turn over and scramble a few times and serve.

Stir-fried Sliced Pork with Mushrooms and Dried Mushrooms

¾ pound lean pork
2½ tablespoons soy sauce
4 dried mushrooms (optional but preferable)
8 medium-size mushrooms
2 tablespoons vegetable oil

1 tablespoon butter
1 teaspoon sugar
2 tablespoons sherry
½ tablespoon cornstarch, blended in 4 tablespoons Broth

Cut pork with sharp knife into 1½-by-1-inch very thin slices. Add 1½ tablespoons soy sauce to it to soak for a few minutes. Soak dried mushrooms in ¼ cup warm water for 20 minutes (retain water) and remove stems. Remove stems from fresh mushrooms and wash thoroughly.

Heat 2 tablespoons oil in a large frying pan. Add pork and stir-fry over high heat for 2½ minutes and push to one side of the pan. Add butter and follow with mushrooms. Stir-fry together both types of mushrooms for 1 minute. Add the remaining soy sauce, sugar, sherry. Mix and scramble the sliced pork together with the mushrooms for 1 minute. Pour in half the mushroom water, and the cornstarch mixture. Stir and scramble together. Soon after the contents reboil and thicken, dish out and serve.

Stir-fried Sliced Pork with Cabbage

¾ pound lean pork
½ pound cabbage (Chinese
   or savoy)
4 tablespoons vegetable oil
1 clove garlic, crushed
1½ teaspoons salt

1½ teaspoons sugar
2 tablespoons sherry
½ tablespoon cornstarch,
   blended in 4 tablespoons
   Broth

Cut pork into very thin slices 2½ by 1½ inches. Cut cabbage into similar-size pieces, discarding coarser parts.

Heat 2 tablespoons oil in a large frying pan. Add pork, garlic and half the salt. Stir-fry over high heat for 2 minutes. Push pork to the sides of the pan. Add remaining oil to the middle of the pan. Pour in the cabbage. Stir-fry over high heat for 1½ minutes. Add sugar, remaining salt and sherry. Bring the pork in from the sides and scramble and fry together for 2 minutes over moderate heat. Add the cornstarch mixture. Turn and scramble together a few times. Allow the contents to heat for a further 2 minutes under cover over moderate heat.

Give them a final 10 seconds stir-fry (adjust for seasoning, or add a few drops more of sherry) and serve.

Stir-fried Sliced Pork with Cucumber

Repeat the preceding recipe, substituting sliced cucumber for cabbage. The last heating together before the final stir-fry can, however, be reduced from 2 minutes to 1 minute.

Minced Pork Dishes

Stuffed Sweet Peppers

4 large sweet peppers
2 tablespoons vegetable oil
1 chili pepper, chopped
1 teaspoon chopped capers
1 clove garlic, chopped
2 teaspoons chopped chives
　or scallion
¼ pound minced lean pork

1 tablespoon soy sauce
1½ teaspoons sugar
¾ tablespoon cornstarch,
　mixed in 3 tablespoons
　Broth
1 tablespoon sherry
2 tablespoons chopped ham
1 tablespoon chopped parsley

Slice off one-third of the top of each pepper, and chop into a fine mince, discarding stem. Scrape out the soft insides of the peppers.

Heat oil in a frying pan. Add chopped chili pepper, capers, garlic, chives and chopped sweet pepper. Stir-fry together for half a minute. Add minced pork and stir-fry together for 2 minutes. Add soy sauce, sugar, cornstarch mixture, and sherry. Stir-fry together for 1½ minutes. Stuff the cooked minced meat and ingredients into the four large sweet peppers. Arrange the peppers on a heatproof dish. Insert the latter into an oven preheated to 400 degrees for 15 minutes. Sprinkle top of minced meat with chopped ham and parsley and serve.

Minced Porkballs with Cabbage
(*Chinese or Savoy*)

¾ pound minced pork
1 tablespoon finely chopped
   chives
2½ tablespoons cornstarch
½ beaten egg
2 tablespoons soy sauce

1 pound cabbage
1 cup Broth
2 tablespoons sherry
1½ teaspoons salt
Pepper to taste

Mix pork, chives, cornstarch, egg and soy sauce into a paste and form paste into 6 to 8 balls.

Chop cabbage into 2-inch pieces. Place at the bottom of a casserole. Pour in Broth and sherry, add pepper and sprinkle with salt. Arrange the porkballs on top of the cabbage. Close the lid of the casserole and insert into an oven preheated at 375 degrees for 1 hour. Serve by bringing the casserole to the table.

Steamed Minced Pork Pudding
with Cauliflower

1 egg
1 pound minced pork
2 tablespoons cornstarch
1½ tablespoons soy sauce
3 teaspoons chopped pickles

1 medium-size cauliflower
½ teaspoon salt
Pepper to taste
2 tablespoons sherry

Beat egg and mix with minced pork, cornstarch, soy sauce,

and chopped pickles into a "paste." Break the cauliflower into individual branches. Pack the branches at the bottom of a large, deep, heatproof basin. Sprinkle with salt, pepper and sherry. Pack minced-pork paste in a thick layer over the cauliflower, sealing all the sides. Cover the top of basin with tinfoil and place the basin in a large saucepan or boiler, standing in about 1½ inches of boiling water. Steam or double-boil the contents for 1 hour and serve in the original basin or heatproof dish. Add boiling water to boiler when necessary.

9

Beef

As there are practically no dairy farms in China, the cows and oxen being regarded as beasts of burden, beef is not as widely used as pork. However, in the areas of China bordering on Manchuria, Inner Mongolia and Sinkiang, which are mostly grasslands, cattle raising is one of the principal activities. Beef is, therefore, a commoner dish in the North and frontier regions than in the South. But this does not mean that beef dishes are not obtainable everywhere in China. There are, in fact, quite a number of them. And practically all the pork dishes can be reproduced in beef, although with beef the long-cooked dishes require longer cooking and the quick-cooked dishes shorter cooking than with pork. Let us start with a few quick-cooked dishes.

Quick-fried Ribbons of Beef with Onions

1½ pounds beefsteak (fillet
  or rump)
2 large onions
2½ tablespoons soy sauce
2 tablespoons sherry
2 teaspoons sugar
¼ teaspoon Tabasco

½ tablespoon shredded ginger
  root (or shedded lemon-
  peel shavings)
1 tablespoon cornstarch
  blended into 2 tablespoons
  chicken stock
4 tablespoons vegetable oil

Shred beef by slicing with a sharp knife into strips or ribbons
1½ inches by ½ inch. Cut onions into very thin slices. Mix
all the seasonings and cornstarch mixture in a large bowl. Add
the shredded beef and work the sauce into the beef with fingers. Leave to stand for a few minutes to half an hour.

Heat the oil in a large frying pan. When very hot add the
onions and stir-fry quickly over high heat for 2 minutes. Push
it to the sides of the pan. Pour the meat into the center of the
pan. Stir-fry, spread it out, and scramble for 1½ minutes over
high heat. Bring in the onions from the sides of the pan to mix
and scramble together with the beef for ¾ minute. Dish out
onto a well-heated serving dish and serve immediately.

Quick-fried Ribbons of Beef with Green Peas

1 small package frozen peas
¾ pound beefsteak
2 teaspoons cornstarch
Pepper to taste
1½ tablespoons soy sauce

2½ tablespoons vegetable oil
½ teaspoon salt
2 tablespoons Broth
2 teaspoons sugar
2 tablespoons sherry

Thaw peas. Shred beef into ribbons, sprinkle with cornstarch, and pepper and add soy sauce to soak for 1 minute.

Heat oil in a large frying pan. When hot add beef to stir-fry for half a minute. Pour in the peas, and all the other ingredients. Continue to stir-fry together over high heat for 1½ minutes. Serve to be eaten piping hot.

Quick-fried Ribbons of Beef with Bean Sprouts

¾ to 1 pound beefsteak	4 tablespoons vegetable oil
2 teaspoons cornstarch	2 cups bean sprouts
1 teaspoon sugar	1 teaspoon salt
Pepper to taste	2 tablespoons Broth
2 tablespoons soy sauce	2 tablespoons sherry

Cut beef into shreds, sprinkle with cornstarch, sugar and pepper, and add soy sauce to soak and rub together for 1 minute. Heat 2 tablespoons oil in a large saucepan. When very hot add the bean sprouts, salt and stir-fry at high heat for 2 minutes. Remove and keep warm.

Add remaining oil, then beef, and stir-fry at high heat for ½ minute. Return the bean sprouts to the pan, add Broth and sherry and stir-fry together for a further minute. Serve to be eaten immediately.

Quick-friend Ribbons of Beef with Young Leeks

Repeat the preceding recipe, substituting 1 cup shredded leeks for bean sprouts. Stir-fry them 3 minutes longer over high heat in the initial frying.

Quick-fried Sliced Beef with Mushrooms

1 pound beefsteak
½ tablespoon cornstarch
Pepper to taste
1½ tablespoons soy sauce
3 tablespoons vegetable oil
6 large mushrooms, cleaned,
   destemmed and quartered
4 dried mushrooms
   soaked in 4 tablespoons
   warm water for ½ hour
and destemmed (optional
   but preferable)
2 tablespoons sherry
3 teaspoons cornstarch,
   blended in 3 tablespoons
   Broth
1½ teaspoons sugar
½ teaspoon salt

Slice beef into very thin slices 1½ inches by ½ inch. Sprinkle with cornstarch and pepper. Add soy sauce to soak and rub into the meat.

Heat oil in a large frying pan. When hot add beef to stir-fry over high heat for 1 minute. Pour in the mushrooms to stir-fry together for 1 minute. Add all the seasonings and ingredients (including 3 tablespoons mushroom liquor from soaking dried mushrooms) and continue to stir-fry over high heat for 1 minute. Serve piping hot.

Quick-fried Sliced Beef with Sweet Peppers

1 pound beefsteak	1 small chopped chili pepper
½ tablespoon cornstarch	(optional)
Pepper to taste	2 teaspoons sugar
1½ tablespoons soy sauce	2 tablespoons sherry
3 medium-size sweet peppers	½ teaspoon salt
3 tablespoons vegetable oil	2 tablespoons Broth

Slice beef into 1½-by-1-inch very thin slices. Sprinkle with cornstarch and pepper. Add soy sauce to soak and rub into meat.

Cut sweet peppers into pieces about the same size as the beef.

Heat 2 tablespoons oil in a large frying pan. Add peppers and chili pepper to stir-fry together over high heat for 1 minute. Remove and keep warm.

Add remaining oil to the pan. Pour in the beef, and stir-fry over high heat for 1 minute. Return the peppers; stir-fry together for half a minute. Add all the seasonings and ingredients and continue to stir-fry together for another minute. Serve to be eaten piping hot.

Quick-fried Sliced Beef with Celery

Repeat the preceding recipe, substituting 1½ cups celery (well cleaned and cut to 1½-by-1-inch segments) for sweet peppers, and stir-fry for 2 minutes instead of 1 minute in the initial frying.

Quick-fried Sliced Beef with Cabbage

Repeat the recipe for Quick-fried Sliced Beef with Sweet Peppers, substituting Chinese celery cabbage or savoy cabbage (using only the tenderer parts) for sweet peppers.

Quick-fried Sliced Beef with Kidneys

1 pound beefsteak
1 pound beef kidney or pig kidney
Pepper to taste
1 tablespoon cornstarch
4 tablespoons Gunpowder Sauce
4 tablespoons vegetable oil
1 clove garlic, crushed

2 stalks spring onion (1-inch segments)
2 tablespoons sherry
3 teaspoons cornstarch, blended in 3 tablespoons Broth
1 teaspoon sugar
½ teaspoon salt

Slice beef into very thin slices, 1½ inches by 1 inch. Remove core and membrane of kidney and cut into similar thin slices. Sprinkle both with pepper and cornstarch and add equal amount of Gunpowder Sauce to rub in and marinate for 5 minutes.

Heat 2 tablespoons oil in a frying pan. Add garlic and kidney to stir-fry for 1½ minutes. Remove and put aside.

Heat remaining oil in the pan. Add beef. Stir-fry over high heat for half a minute. Add spring onion. Return kidney to the pan. Add sherry, cornstarch mixture, sugar and salt. Continue to stir-fry together over high heat for 1½ minutes and serve immediately.

Quick-fried Sliced Beef with Oysters

Beef is often cooked with oyster sauce in China, especially in Canton. As oyster sauce is no more easily available in the West than fresh oysters, we might as well cook with oysters, as we used to do in my province, Fukien.

1 pound beefsteak
Pepper to taste
  2 tablespoons Gunpowder
    Sauce
  2 teaspoons chopped chives
  2 teaspoons lemon rind,
    finely chopped
  ½ teaspoon salt
Paprika to taste
  4 tablespoons sherry
  12 oysters, cleaned and shelled,
    (retain oyster liquor)

4 tablespoons vegetable oil
2 cloves garlic, crushed
3 stalks spring onion (1-inch
  segments)
3 teaspoons cornstarch,
  blended in 3 tablespoons
  Broth
2 teaspoons lemon juice
1½ tablespoons chopped
  parsley

Slice beef into 1½-by-1-inch thin slices. Pepper and soak in Gunpowder Sauce to marinate for 5 minutes.

Add chives, chopped lemon rind, salt, paprika and 2 tablespoons sherry to oysters to marinate for 5 minutes.

Heat 2 tablespoons oil in a large frying pan over moderate heat. Add garlic and then pour in the oysters. Stir-fry gently (so that the oysters do not break) for ¾ minute. Remove and keep warm.

Add remaining oil to the pan and turn heat up to high. Add the marinated beef and spring onions. Stir-fry for 1 minute. Return the oysters to the pan, along with blended cornstarch and remaining sherry. Stir-fry together over moderate heat gently for 1 minute. Sprinkle with lemon juice and chopped parsley. Serve to be eaten piping hot.

Red-cooked Beef

4 to 5 pounds beef (shin or shank)	Bouquet garni (1 small cloth bag of herbs)
2 cups Gunpowder Sauce	6 tablespoons sherry

Boil beef in a panful of water for 10 minutes, pour away water. Transfer beef to a casserole. Pour Gunpowder Sauce over the beef, turning the meat around in the sauce a few times. Add bouquet garni and sherry. Close lid of the casserole firmly and place in an oven preheated to 375 degrees for 1 hour. Reduce to 300 degrees for approximately 2 hours, turning the beef over every half hour. Remove bouquet garni. Slice beef and serve with its gravy.

This beef is equally good served cold. The recipe is intended to serve two or three people for more than one meal, or for a party of up to ten people.

Chopped Red-cooked Beef with Carrots or Turnips

2 to 3 pounds stewing beef	2 cups carrots, cleaned and cut in wedge shape
1 cup Gunpowder Sauce	
4 tablespoons sherry	

Cut beef into 2-by-1-by-1-inch oblong pieces. Boil beef in a panful of water for 10 minutes. Pour away water and transfer beef to a casserole. Add half the Gunpowder Sauce. Stir and turn the beef around in the sauce a few times. Insert the casserole in a preheated oven at 350 degrees for ¾ hour. Add the sherry, carrots and remainder of Gunpowder Sauce. Turn the beef and carrots around in the sauce a few times and return the casserole to the oven at the same temperature for 15 minutes. Reduce temperature to 325 degrees, heat for another 50 minutes and serve in the original casserole.

10

Lamb

LAMB, like beef, is a favorite food of North China and the frontier territories, which are near to the cattle- and sheep-raising grasslands. As lamb or mutton is considered even stronger in flavor than beef, it is usually cooked with strong-flavored ingredients such as leeks, onions, scallions, garlic, ginger, various herbs, Wine Sediment Paste and plentiful wine.

Quick-fried Sliced Lamb with Spring Onions

1½ pounds lamb (leg)
½ tablespoon cornstarch
3 tablespoons soy sauce
½ teaspoon Tabasco

2 tablespoons sherry
6 stalks spring onion
3 tablespoons vegetable oil
1 clove garlic, crushed

Slice lamb into thin pieces 2 inches by 1 inch. Sprinkle with cornstarch, soy sauce, Tabasco and sherry. Work the ingredients into the meat with fingers. Cut spring onions into 1½-inch segments.

Heat oil in a large frying pan. When hot add lamb and garlic and stir-fry over high heat for 3 minutes. Add spring onions, and stir-fry together for another minute. Serve on well-heated dish; to be eaten immediately.

Quick-fried Sliced Lamb with Young Leeks

Repeat the preceding recipe, substituting young leeks for onions (1 cup leeks chopped to 1½-inch segments), except that the leeks should be added to the lamb after the meat has been stir-fried for 1 minute only. Stir-fry lamb and leeks together for 3 minutes.

Quick-fried Sliced Lamb with Onion

Repeat the recipe for Quick-fried Sliced Lamb with Spring Onions, substituting 2 large onions (thinly sliced) for the spring onions. Stir-fry the onions together with lamb and garlic from the beginning with 1 additional tablespoon of oil, 1 tablespoon soy sauce, I teaspoon sugar and 2 tablespoons Broth.

Triple-quick-fries

1 pound lamb (leg)
½ pound lamb kidney (after removing core, membrane, etc.)
½ pound lamb liver
3 tablespoons soy sauce
5 tablespoons sherry
1½ tablespoons cornstarch
4 tablespoons vegetable oil
2 cloves garlic, crushed
2 tablespoons finely chopped onion
1 teaspoon sugar
2 tablespoons Broth
1 tablespoon chopped parsley

Slice lamb into thin slices 2 inches by 1 inch. Slice kidney and liver into similar thin slices. Add 1 tablespoon soy sauce and 1 tablespoon sherry to each type of meat separately. Sprinkle with cornstarch and work in the seasonings with fingers.

Stir-fry each type of meat, one after another, separately, in 1 tablespoon oil (use 2 tablespoons for initial frying of lamb) for 1 minute and put aside. Finally, stir-fry the garlic and onion in the remaining oil in the same frying pan for ¼ minute and return all the meats to the pan for a final stir-fry together, adding the remaining sherry, sugar and Broth for 2 minutes, over high heat.

Triple-quick-fries with Wine Sediment Paste

Repeat the preceding recipe, substituting 2 tablespoons Wine Sediment Paste for the final 2 tablespoons sherry. The Wine Sediment Paste should be added to the pan, along with garlic and onion, at the beginning of the final stir-fry with 1 tablespoon additional oil.

Portions: The following lamb dishes will serve up to nine persons, or may be used for more than one meal.

Red-cooked Lamb

3 to 4 pounds mutton	1 tablespoon soy sauce
4 cups boiling water	2 cloves garlic, crushed
6 tablespoons Gunpowder	1 bouquet garni
Sauce	4 tablespoons sherry
1 cup Broth	

Chop lamb into 1½-inch cubes. Add them to boiling water in a heavy saucepan to simmer for 5 minutes. Pour away two-thirds the water and impurities. Add the remaining ingredients. Simmer very gently for 1¾ hours, turning meat over now and then. Remove bouquet garni. Serve in a tureen or deep-sided dish.

Stewed Lamb in Wine Sediment Paste

Repeat the recipe for Red-cooked Lamb, using only 3 tablespoons Gunpowder Sauce. Add 4 tablespoons Wine Sediment Paste during last half-hour of cooking.

Stewed Lamb in Wine with Turnips

Repeat recipe for Red-cooked Lamb. Pour away all the water after the initial boiling. Add 2 cups white wine and all the other seasonings and ingredients, together with 2 cups turnips, cut into ax-head or wedge-shaped pieces, 1½ inches long. Simmer gently for 1¼ to 1¾ hours. Adjust for seasonings and serve.

Quick-fried Shredded Lamb with Shredded Vegetables

1 pound lamb	3 stalks spring onion (in
2 teaspoons cornstarch	1-inch segments)
1½ tablespoons soy sauce	1 cup bean sprouts
2 tablespoons sherry	½ teaspoon salt
4 tablespoons vegetable oil	2 tablespoons Wine Sediment
1 cup shredded celery	Paste (optional)

Slice lamb into thin shredded strips. Sprinkle with cornstarch. Add soy sauce and sherry, and work in with fingers.

Heat 2 tablespoons oil in a large frying pan. Add lamb and stir-fry over high heat for 2 minutes, then put lamb aside.

Add remaining oil to the pan. Add celery and spring onion to stir-fry together for 1 minute over high heat. Pour in the bean sprouts and salt. Stir-fry together for ½ minute. Push all the vegetables to the sides of the pan. Add Wine Sediment Paste to the center of the pan. Stir it in the oil for a few seconds (if no oil left, add 1 tablespoon). Return the shredded lamb to the pan. Stir-fry the vegetables and meat together for 1 minute and serve.

Quick-dipped Lamb

This is a kind of Chinese lamb fondue, which has to be cooked in a chafing dish (whether heated by charcoal, methylated spirits or electric fry) on the dining table. The shape of the dish or pan has to be wide open, and at least 3 to 4 inches deep and 10 to 12 inches in diameter, so that it will contain at least 4 to 6 cups of Broth kept at rolling boil. (Preferably equipped with lid — a large round casserole sitting on electric heater should serve the purpose.)

4 pounds lamb	2 pints Broth
3 stalks spring onion	1 package egg noodles
2 cups cabbage or celery	

Portions: For such a dish or meal the minimum amount of lamb should be calculated at ½ to 1 pound per person. For a party this main dish should be complemented by a couple of other quick-fried dishes to be eaten with a small amount of rice.

Slice lamb into paper-thin slices approximately 2½-by-1½-inch size. Divide into six plates and place on dining table.

Cut spring onion into 1½-inch segments, celery or cabbage into 1½-inch pieces. Place cabbage on two plates and onion on one plate on the table.

Heat Broth in kitchen and bring it to the table in the chafing dish (or casserole) just off boil, with some onion and cabbage added. The fire under the dish should burn briskly.

Each diner will then use his or her chopsticks to pick up a piece of lamb and dip it into the boiling Broth for not more than 1 to 1½ minutes, and then retrieve it to plunge into one of the following dips before eating:

Soy and vinegar dip (2 tablespoons soy sauce mixed
  with 3 tablespoons vinegar)
Soy and sherry dip (2 tablespoons soy sauce and 3 table-
  spoons sherry)
Soy chili dip (3 tablespoons soy sauce and 3 teaspoons
  Tabasco)
Tomato sauce
Mustard
Plum Sauce

When nearly all the lamb is consumed the diner will add all
the remaining cabbage and onion to the now enriched Broth
along with noodles. The lid is then placed on the chafing dish
to allow the vegetable and noodles to cook under cover for
five minutes. Whereupon each diner will fill his own bowl
with a ladleful of this excellent soup and noodles from the
chafing dish, and complete the meal with a hot "wash-down."

11

Chicken

CHICKEN, like pork, is considered in China a very versatile meat; it is able to combine successfully with a great number of other food materials to produce a vast number of dishes. Often, too, it is cooked and prepared with distinction as a dish on its own without entering into any marriages or combinations. Like the majority of meats, it is presented in the usual varieties of size or shape: cooked as a whole bird, chopped into large pieces, cut into slices, diced into cubes or shredded into threads; and within each type of preparation it has its own traditions and its traditional types of food with which to combine. As a rule, the smaller the chicken the shorter the time it requires to cook, but somewhat longer time is required to prepare it; and on the other hand, chicken which is cooked

whole, or in large pieces, usually takes very little time to prepare but much longer to cook.

Diced Chicken Quick-fried in Soy Sauce

2 breasts of chicken
3 teaspoons cornstarch
2 tablespoons soy sauce
2 tablespoons vegetable oil
1 tablespoon finely chopped
  onion

1 clove garlic, crushed and
  chopped
2 teaspoons tomato purée
½ teaspoon sugar
1 teaspoon vinegar
1 tablespoon sherry

Dice chicken into ½-inch cubes. Place in a bowl. Sprinkle
with cornstarch and soy sauce. Work them in with fingers.

Heat oil in a frying pan. Add onion and garlic and stir-fry
together over high heat for ½ minute. Add purée, sugar,
vinegar and sherry. Continue to stir-fry for ¼ minute. Pour
in the chicken. Spread it out on the pan. Stir-fry quickly for
1¼ minutes and serve at once; to be eaten hot.

Diced Chicken Quick-fried in Sweet and Sour Sauce

2 breasts of chicken
½ teaspoon salt
½ tablespoon cornstarch
3 tablespoons vegetable oil
1 tablespoon finely chopped
  onion

1 clove garlic, crushed and
  chopped
5 tablespoons Sweet and Sour
  Sauce

Dice chicken into ½-inch cubes. Rub with salt and cornstarch.

Heat 2 tablespoons oil in a frying pan. When very hot add chicken cubes and stir-fry quickly for 1 minute. Remove and put aside. Add remaining oil, onion and garlic. Stir-fry together for ½ minute. Add the Sweet and Sour Sauce. Continue to mix and fry together for 10 to 15 seconds. Return the chicken cubes to the pan. Mix and stir-fry in the "sauce" for ½ minute and serve.

Diced Chicken Quick-fried in Hot Sauce

Repeat the preceding recipe, substituting the following sauce mixture for the Sweet and Sour Sauce.

1 tablespoon soy sauce	2 teaspoons vinegar
½ teaspoon salt	½ tablespoon cornstarch,
1 tablespoon tomato purée	blended in 2 tablespoons
1½ teaspoons Tabasco	Broth
1 tablespoon sherry	

This is obviously a "hot" dish.

Diced Chicken Quick-fried with Walnuts

2 breasts of chicken	1 teaspoon soy sauce
1 cup walnut meats	2 tablespoons Broth
1 teaspoon salt	1 teaspoon sugar
½ tablespoon cornstarch	2 tablespoons sherry
4 tablespoons vegetable oil	

Dice chicken into ¼- to ½-inch cubes. Cut walnut meats into

similar-size pieces. Rub chicken with salt and cornstarch.

Heat 2 tablespoons oil in a frying pan. Pour in the walnut meats and stir-fry over moderate heat for 3 minutes. Remove and keep warm.

Add 1 tablespoon oil to the pan. Add the chicken cubes. Stir-fry over high heat for ½ minute. Add remaining oil, soy sauce, Broth, sugar and sherry. Return the walnuts to the pan, continue to stir-fry over high heat for 1 minute and serve.

Diced Chicken with Sweet Peppers and Chili Peppers

2 breasts of chicken
2 green or red sweet peppers
2 red chili peppers
¼ teaspoon salt
2 teaspoons cornstarch
3 tablespoons vegetable oil
1 clove garlic, crushed and
   chopped

2 tablespoons soy sauce
2 tablespoons sherry
2 tablespoons Broth
2 teaspoons vinegar
1 teaspoon sugar

This is another "hot" dish.

Dice chicken into ½-inch cubes and sweet peppers into similar-size squares. Chop chili peppers into ¼-inch pieces; remove and discard pips. Rub chicken with salt and corn-starch.

Heat 2 tablespoons oil in a frying pan. When hot pour in the chicken for half-minute stir-fry. Remove and keep warm.

Add remaining oil to the pan. Add garlic, both types of peppers, and stir-fry them over high heat for 1½ minutes. Add soy sauce, sherry, Broth, vinegar and sugar. Stir-fry for

5 seconds. Return the chicken to the pan, continue to stir-fry for 2 minutes and serve.

Diced Chicken Quick-fried with Cucumber and Button Mushrooms

2 breasts of chicken	1 tablespoon soy sauce
1 6-inch section of a large cucumber	1 cup button mushrooms
	2 tablespoons Broth
½ teaspoon salt	1½ teaspoons sugar
3 teaspoons cornstarch	Pepper to taste
3 tablespoons vegetable oil	2 tablespoons sherry

Dice chicken into ½-inch cubes. Clean cucumber thoroughly without peeling; cut into pieces similar to the chicken cubes. Rub chicken with salt and cornstarch.

Heat 2 tablespoons oil in the frying pan. Add chicken and stir-fry over moderate heat for 1 minute. Remove and keep warm.

Add remaining oil to the pan. Pour in the cucumber and mushrooms. Stir-fry over high heat for 1 minute. Add the remaining ingredients. Return chicken to the pan. Stir-fry together for 1 minute and serve.

Diced Chicken with Shrimps or Lobsters

Repeat preceding recipe, substituting 6 tablespoons Fu Yung Sauce and ½ teaspoon salt for soy sauce, and adding ½ cup shrimps when mushrooms are added. This is an extremely tasty party dish often called "Stir-fried Phoenix and Dragon" — chicken being the Phoenix and seafood the Dragon. If lobsters or giant shrimps are used they should be reduced to more or less the same size pieces as the diced chicken.

Diced Chicken with Frozen Peas

1 breast of chicken	1 package frozen peas
½ teaspoon salt	2 tablespoons Broth
Pepper to taste	2 teaspoons soy sauce
2 teaspoons cornstarch	1 teaspoon sugar
2 tablespoons oil	2 tablespoons sherry

Dice chicken breast into ½-inch cubes. Sprinkle with salt, pepper and dust with cornstarch. Heat oil in a frying pan. When hot add chicken and stir-fry for 20 to 25 seconds. Remove pan from heat, but keep hot.

Thaw peas, heat them in a small saucepan with 2 tablespoons Broth, soy sauce, sugar, 2 tablespoons sherry. Allow them to simmer together for 3 minutes.

Pour the peas and gravy into the frying pan with the chicken. Turn the heat up to the maximum, stir-fry together for 25 seconds and serve in a well-heated bowl.

Shredded Chicken

When the breast of chicken has been used, the remainder of the meat is scraped from the bones with a sharp knife and usually shredded. (For easier scraping and shredding, boil the chicken for 5 minutes.) It is then often stir-fried with vegetables which are threadlike in shape, which makes them particularly suitable for combining with or garnishing noodles or other foods also in lengthwise pieces.

Shredded Chicken Quick-fried with Bean Sprouts

1 breast of chicken	2 cups bean sprouts
½ teaspoon salt	1 tablespoon soy sauce
2 teaspoons cornstarch	2 tablespoons Broth
3 tablespoons vegetable oil	1 tablespoon vinegar
2 stalks spring onion (1-inch segments)	2 tablespoons sherry
	Pepper to taste

Shred chicken meat into thin ribbons. Rub with salt and cornstarch.

Heat 2 tablespoons oil in a frying pan. Add chicken. Stir-fry for ½ minute. Remove and keep warm.

Add remaining oil to the pan with spring onions. Stir-fry for ¼ minute. Add bean sprouts. Stir-fry over high heat for 1 minute. Add all remaining seasonings and ingredients. Stir-fry for another ½ minute. Finally, return the chicken to the pan, stir-fry all together for another ¾ minute and serve.

Shredded Chicken with Celery

Repeat the preceding recipe, substituting 2 cups celery (shredded to the same size as the ribbons of chicken) for bean sprouts, and add 1 teaspoon Tabasco for vinegar.

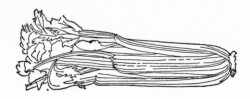

Shredded Chicken Quick-fried with Shredded Mushrooms and Bamboo Shoots

1 breast of chicken
½ teaspoon salt
2 teaspoons cornstarch
3 tablespoons vegetable oil
2 stalks spring onion (1-inch segments)
1 cup shredded mushrooms

1 cup shredded bamboo shoots
1 tablespoon soy sauce
2 tablespoons Broth
3 tablespoons mushroom liquor
2 tablespoons sherry
Pepper to taste

Shred chicken meat into thin ribbons. Rub with salt and cornstarch. Heat 2 tablespoons oil in frying pan. Add chicken. Stir-fry for ½ minute. Remove and keep warm. Add remaining oil to pan with spring onions. Stir-fry for ½ minute. Add bamboo shoots; stir-fry for ½ minute; add mushrooms, and stir-fry for ½ minute, then add remaining ingredients. Finally, add chicken for assembly fry of 1 ½ minutes.

Shredded Chicken with Sweet Pepper and Chili Pepper Ribbons

For those who prefer their food "hot" this is a good dish to prepare. Repeat recipe for Shredded Chicken Quick-fried with Bean Sprouts, substituting 2 large sweet peppers (shredded) for bean sprouts and 1 to 2 chili peppers (shredded) for spring onion; but since the dish is extremely "hot" the addition of 1 chili pepper is sufficient for most people.

Sliced Chicken

Sliced chicken differs from shredded chicken in that it is usually cooked with larger cuts or large pieces of vegetables, which every now and then require a brief period of parboiling before stir-frying together. Sliced chicken is best prepared from breast of chicken or chicken legs (both without skin).

Sliced Chicken Quick-fried with Cauliflower

1 breast of chicken	3 tablespoons vegetable oil
2 teaspoons cornstarch	1 tablespoon soy sauce
1 teaspoon salt	4 tablespoons Broth
1 small cauliflower	2 tablespoons sherry

Slice chicken meat with a sharp knife into very thin pieces approximately 1 inch by ¾ inch. Rub with cornstarch and half the salt. Break cauliflower into individual branches approximately 1½ inches by 1 inch. Parboil in water for 5 minutes and drain.

Heat 2 tablespoons oil in a frying pan. When hot add chicken to stir-fry for ½ minute. Remove and keep warm. Add remaining oil and cauliflower. Stir-fry for ½ minute. Sprinkle with remaining salt and soy sauce. Add Broth. Turn the cauliflower over in the sauce a few times. Close the top of the frying pan with a lid, and allow the contents to simmer over moderate heat for 2 minutes. Return the chicken to the pan. Add sherry and stir-fry over high heat for ½ minute and serve.

Sliced Chicken Quick-fried with Broccoli

Repeat the preceding recipe, substituting broccoli for cauliflower.

Sliced Chicken Quick-fried with Mushrooms

1 breast of chicken	2 tablespoons butter
½ teaspoon salt	1 tablespoon soy sauce
2 teaspoons cornstarch	2 tablespoons Broth
8 large mushrooms	½ tablespoon cornstarch,
6 dried mushrooms (optional	blended with 3 tablespoons
but preferable)	mushroom liquor
2 tablespoons vegetable oil	2 tablespoons sherry

Slice chicken into very thin slices, about 1 inch by ¾ inch.

Rub with salt and cornstarch. Destem and clean mushrooms thoroughly. Soak dried mushrooms in 6 tablespoons warm water for 30 minutes (destem, and retain 3 tablespoons water).

Heat oil in a frying pan. Add chicken and stir-fry over high heat for ½ minute. Remove and put aside.

Add butter and mushrooms. Stir-fry together for 1 minute. Add soy sauce, Broth, cornstarch blended in mushroom liquor, and sherry. Continue to stir-fry for 1 minute. Return chicken to the pan, stir-fry all contents together for another ½ minute and serve.

Sliced Chicken Quick-fried with Pig's Liver

1 breast of chicken	4 tablespoons vegetable oil
¼ teaspoon salt	1 clove garlic, chopped
1 tablespoon cornstarch	2 stalks spring onion (1-inch
½ pound pig's liver	segments)
1 teaspoon sugar	1½ tablespoons Gunpowder
1 tablespoon soy sauce	Sauce
½ tablespoon vinegar	1½ tablespoons sherry

Slice chicken into thin slices, 1½ inches by ¼ inch. Rub with salt and half the cornstarch. Cut pig's liver into similar slices and rub with remaining cornstarch; sprinkle and rub with sugar, soy sauce and vinegar and leave to marinate for ¼ hour.

Heat 2 tablespoons oil in a frying pan. When hot add chicken and stir-fry for ½ minute. Remove and keep warm.

Add remaining oil to the pan. Add garlic and spring onion. Stir-fry for ¼ minute. Pour in the sliced liver. Continue to stir-fry over moderate heat for 2 minutes. Return the chicken to the pan. Pour in the Gunpowder Sauce and sherry. Stir-fry together over high heat for ¾ minute and serve.

Sliced Chicken Quick-fried with Pineapple

Repeat the preceding recipe, substituting one small can of pineapple for dried mushrooms. Cut each slice of pineapple into 4 wedges, reserving juice. They should be added to stir-fry when the mushrooms are added. Quarter of the pineapple juice should then be added into 6 tablespoons Sweet and Sour Sauce, which should replace the various seasonings and ingredients used in the last stage of cooking in the preceding recipe.

Chopped Chicken

In China chicken is often served chopped into sixteen to twenty pieces. When prepared in such a manner the chicken is more often than not cooked on its own, without supplementary materials, and with only flavoring ingredients. It is usually cooked by stir-frying, deep-frying, braising or red-cooking. Because of the fact that it is not combined with other foods or materials, there is a certain simplicity about this way of cooking chicken — except you will need a sharp chopper to chop up the birds (through the bones) at the beginning, and you will need to be adept at stripping the meat from the bones in your mouth when eating it.

Portions: For six to nine persons, or for more than one meal.

Chopped, Salted, Deep-fried Chicken

In China deep-fry does not necessarily mean frying in a deep-fryer. It can be done in an ordinary frying pan with lid, or a large saucepan, except you will have to turn the pieces of chicken or other food over and over in hot oil.

1 2-pound roaster or pullet	1 tablespoon chopped onion
2½ teaspoons salt	2 tablespoons sherry
1 tablespoon lemon rind, finely chopped	½ cup vegetable oil

For batter:

4 tablespoons flour	4 tablespoons milk or water
1 egg	

Chop chicken through the bone into 20 regular pieces. Sprinkle with salt, lemon rind, onion and sherry. Rub the ingredients into the pieces of chicken with fingers. Let stand for ½ hour.

Meanwhile, make batter by blending the batter ingredients together into a consistent mixture.

Heat oil in a large saucepan. Dip the chicken in the batter. Add a few pieces to the pan at a time (protect yourself with the lid from splattering oil). When all the chicken has been added to the pan, and the splattering has reduced, turn the pieces of chicken over with a pair of bamboo chopsticks or perforated spoon. Fry over high heat for 2½ to 3 minutes. Drain and serve to be eaten hot.

Small saucedishes of tomato sauce, or pepper-salt mixture (preferably heated together for one minute on a dry pan) should be provided on the table for diners to dip their pieces of chicken in when eating.

Chopped Braised-fried Chicken in Soy Sauce

1 roaster, 2 to 3 pounds	2 tablespoons sherry
3 tablespoons vegetable oil	1½ tablespoons lard
2 tablespoons chopped onion	2 stalks spring onion (1-inch
1 clove garlic, chopped	segments)
4 tablespoons Broth	3 tablespoons Gunpowder
2 tablespoons soy sauce	Sauce

Chop chicken into 20 regular pieces with a sharp chopper. Heat oil in a large saucepan. Add chopped onion and garlic to stir-fry for 15 seconds. Add the chicken. Stir-fry over high heat for 4 to 5 minutes. Pour in the Broth, soy sauce, sherry. Turn the pieces of chicken over in the sauce a few times. Close the pan with a lid and allow the contents to cook under cover over moderate heat for 5 minutes. By this time, the liquid in the pan will have been very much reduced. Turn the heat high, add lard, spring onion and Gunpowder Sauce. Stir-fry until the chicken is almost completely dried (as if it has been stir-fried only). Pour contents out immediately into a well-heated deep-sided dish and serve.

Chopped Braised-fried Chicken in Wine Sediment Paste

Repeat the preceding recipe, substituting 4 tablespoons Wine Sediment Paste for Gunpowder Sauce, reducing the Broth used to 2 tablespoons, and the braising from 5 minutes to 3 minutes. Lengthen the final stir-fry, so as to enable the chicken to be turned a little longer and more thoroughly in the paste. A highly aromatic dish.

Chopped Red-cooked Chicken

1 4-to-5-pound chicken (hen or capon)	1 cup water
3 tablespoons vegetable oil	½ cup Gunpowder Sauce
2 tablespoons chopped onion	1 tablespoon soy sauce
1 clove garlic, chopped	½ cup sherry
	2 teaspoons sugar

Chop bird into 20 pieces. Heat oil in a heavy saucepan. Add onion and garlic and stir-fry over high heat for ½ minute. Add the chicken and stir-fry together for 3 minutes. Pour in 1 cup water, ¼ cup Gunpower Sauce and 1 tablespoon soy sauce. Turn the chicken over in the liquid a few times. Close the lid and allow contents to simmer over low fire for ¾ hour (turning chicken over once every ¼ hour). Add the sherry, sugar and the remainder of the Gunpowder Sauce. Turn the pieces of chicken over in the liquid a few times and allow them to simmer over very low heat (insert an asbestos sheet under the pan) for another 45 minutes, turning the pieces over every 15 minutes. Serve in a tureen or deep-sided dish.

Crackling, Deep-fried Chopped Chicken

1 3-to-4-pound chicken	4 tablespoons soy sauce
2 teaspoons salt	Oil for deep-fry
½ tablespoon malt (barley) sugar	2 egg whites
	4 tablespoons cornstarch

Chop chicken into 20 regular pieces. Rub thoroughly with salt. Place in a colander over a plate in airy spot to dry for at least 3 hours. Heat sugar in soy sauce until the former has all melted. Allow the mixture to cool.

Heat oil in the deep-fryer. When very hot lower the pieces of chicken in a wire-basket to fry for 2 minutes, remove and drain thoroughly. Pour the sugar–soy sauce mixture over the pieces of chicken placed in a basin. Turn the chicken over in the sauce a few times to insure that every piece is well covered. Dip the chicken pieces now in a mixture of 2 egg whites whisked for 2 minutes with 4 tablespoons cornstarch. Return the chicken for a second period of deep-fry for 1½ to 1¾ minutes. Drain and serve. Chicken cooked in this manner should be eaten dipped in Plum Sauce, or salt-and-pepper mix (heating a mixture of 2 tablespoons salt and 1½ teaspoon pepper in a dry pan over moderate heat for 1 minute).

White-cut Chicken

1 young chicken, 2 to 3 pounds	3 teaspoons salt
4 cups water	3 stalks spring onion

Place chicken in a saucepan. Add water, salt and spring onion chopped to 2-inch segments. Bring to boil and simmer for 20 minutes, turning the chicken over a couple of times. Remove pan from heat. Allow the chicken to cook in remaining heat, under cover, for ½ hour. Remove the chicken from the pan. Let cool and place in the refrigerator for 1 hour. When cold, chop through the bone into 16 to 20 pieces with a sharp knife. The pieces should then be reassembled or arranged neatly on a serving dish. It should be eaten dipped in good-grade soy sauce, soy sauce mixed with vinegar, or soy sauce mixed with sherry or with Tabasco.

Chopped, Simmered Chicken in Fu Yung Sauce

1 chicken, 2 to 3 pounds	4 tablespoons sherry
¼ pound ham	½ cup Broth
¾ pound broccoli	2 cups Fu Yung Sauce
2 teaspoons salt	

Chop chicken through bone into 20 pieces. Cut ham and broccoli into similar-size pieces. Sprinkle chicken with salt and sherry.

Line a casserole with broccoli, place the pieces of chicken on top and pieces of ham on top of the chicken. Sprinkle with Broth and sherry and insert the casserole in an oven preheated to 400 degrees for 40 minutes. Meanwhile heat the Fu Yung Sauce in a large saucepan. When chicken is ready empty the contents of the casserole into the sauce in the saucepan. Turn the chicken, broccoli and ham over in the sauce for 5 minutes, serve in a large bowl, tureen or deep-sided dish.

Chinese Roast Chicken

1 3-pound roaster	2 tablespoons soy sauce
6 tablespoons Gunpowder Sauce	3 tablespoons tangerine or orange peel
3 teaspoons sugar	4 stalks spring onion

Clean and dry chicken thoroughly. Stand it in the oven at 250 degrees for 10 minutes to dry further. Mix the Gunpowder Sauce with sugar and soy sauce in a marinade. Rub the chicken thoroughly with the marinade. Stand it in the latter for 1 hour, turning it over, and rub a few more times. Stuff the bird with orange peel and spring onion cut to 1-inch segments.

Place the chicken in the oven preheated at 400 degrees for 50 minutes, turning the bird over occasionally, and basting a couple of times with remaining marinade (with aid of brush).

Chop the bird with a sharp chopper into 20 pieces and serve; or carve and serve in the normal Western style.

Long-simmered Chicken with Cabbage, Mushrooms and Ham

1 stewing fowl, 3 to 4 pounds	6 large mushrooms
6 cups water	4 dried mushrooms, thoroughly soaked to soften
2 teaspoons salt	3 slices ham or salami
3 cups cabbage	
3 stalks spring onion	

Boil chicken in water for 10 minutes. Pour away two-thirds

of the water. Transfer to a casserole, add salt. Place the casserole in an oven preheated at 350 degrees for ¾ hour, turning the chicken over once. Meanwhile cut cabbage into 2-inch pieces and spring onion into 2-inch segments, destem mushrooms and dried mushrooms and slice into narrow 2-inch strips. Cut salami into similar strips.

Insert the cabbage under the chicken in the casserole and drape the chicken with spring onion, ham or salami and mushrooms. Return the casserole to the oven to continue to cook at 350 degrees for another hour. Serve by bringing the casserole to the table. The chicken should be tender enough to take to pieces with a pair of chopsticks.

Curried Chicken

1 young chicken, 1 to 2 pounds	1 small onion, chopped
2½ teaspoons salt	1 clove garlic, crushed and chopped
5 tablespoons vegetable oil	½ cup Broth
2 tablespoons curry powder	1 tablespoon soy sauce
1 cup young leeks	

Chop chicken through bone into 16 to 20 pieces. Rub with 1½ teaspoons salt. Heat 3 tablespoons oil in a saucepan or sautéing pan, stir-fry chicken slowly over high heat for 10 minutes and remove.

Add curry powder and remaining oil to the pan. Cut leeks to 1-inch segments. Add to the pan along with onion and garlic. Stir-fry over high heat for 1½ minutes. Add remaining salt. Continue to stir-fry for 2 minutes. Pour in the Broth and soy sauce. Stir for 2 to 3 minutes. When boiling return the chicken to the pan. Turn the pieces of chicken in the sauce a few times. Close the lid of the pan firmly and leave contents to simmer gently for the next 20 minutes. Open the lid, turn the contents over once more. Serve in a deep-sided dish.

Jellied Chicken

1 young chicken, 2 to 3 pounds	4 tablespoons sherry
6 to 8 cups water	4 2-inch segments cucumber
2 cups Broth	1 red sweet pepper
1 teaspoon salt	1½ tablespoons gelatin
	Lettuce and parsley for garnish

Boil chicken in water for 35 minutes. Leave to cool in the pan. When cold drain and chop through bone into 16 to 20 pieces.

Heat Broth in a small saucepan. Add salt, sherry, cucumber (do not peel), and pepper diced to 1-inch-square pieces. Simmer for 6 to 7 minutes. Remove the pepper and cucumber with a perforated spoon. Add gelatin to dissolve completely in the Broth.

Meanwhile, arrange chicken, skin side down, in a mold interleaved with the red and green of the sweet pepper and cucumber. Pour the Broth over them, and place the mold in a refrigerator for 3 hours or overnight to set.

When serving unmold the gelatinized chicken and jelly on a serving plate, and set them off by surrounding them with a bank of lettuce, and garnish the whole with a few sprigs of parsley.

Paper-wrapped Chicken

1 large sheet cellophane paper	1 tablespoon soy sauce
1 breast of chicken	1 tablespoon sherry
2 slices bacon	1 teaspoon sugar
1 2-inch section of cucumber	Pepper to taste
2 stalks spring onion	Oil for deep-fry

Cut cellophane paper into pieces 8 by 6 inches. Cut chicken into 12 lengthwise strips 2 by 3 inches. Cut bacon across lean and fat into 12 strips. Cut cucumber vertically into similar strips and spring onion into 12 segments 2 to 3 inches long.

Add soy sauce, sherry and sugar to the chicken. Allow the chicken to soak in the marinade for 10 minutes.

Place a piece of cellophane paper in front of you, with the 8-inch side stretching to your left and right. Place a piece of marinated chicken, horizontally, just below the center of the paper. Add a strip of bacon, spring onion and cucumber. Roll up the pieces from the bottom up, outward (from you) in a loose roll. When you are about 2 inches from the top flatten the roll, so that it looks like a narrow envelope. Turn in the two sides and fold down the flap from the top, tucking it in under the two folded-in sides. Turn the "envelope" over and place a dish on it to keep firm. Use all the materials and pack them into similar envelopes with the eleven remaining pieces of cellophane paper.

When they are all ready, place 6 envelopes at a time in wire basket to deep-fry in very hot oil for 1½ minutes. Remove from oil to rest for 2 minutes and then lower all envelopes for another 1½ minutes of frying. By that time the chicken should be well cooked.

The envelopes should then be well drained, and arranged on a well-heated serving dish, like a trayful of envelopes containing important messages, to be picked up and opened with a pair of chopsticks and eaten by diners from their plates.

Paper-wrapped Chicken with Oyster and Abalone

Repeat the preceding recipe, generously adding 1 oyster, 1 strip abalone (the same size as bacon) and 1 sprig of parsley to each envelope, lengthening the initial frying to 2 minutes.

This is an excellent party dish.

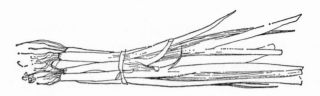

Red-cooked Chicken (whole)

1 stewing fowl, 3 to 4 pounds   1 cup water
1 cup Gunpowder Sauce

Clean and place the chicken in a casserole. Pour the water and Gunpowder Sauce over the chicken. Insert the casserole into an oven at 375 degrees (preheated) for ¾ hour. Turn the chicken over and reduce heat to 325 degrees; cook for another hour, turning the chicken over a few times in the process.

This is a standby home-cooked dish, which requires, as you can see, very little work to prepare and cook.

Drunken Chicken

1 chicken, 2 to 3 pounds   2 bottles dry sherry
6 onions, chopped   2 tablespoons chopped parsley
2 tablespoons salt

Clean chicken. Mix finely chopped onions with salt. Rub chicken inside and out with mixture. Let it stand for 15 minutes. Rub for a second time. Place chicken in an airy place to salt and dry for two days.

After two days rinse it quickly under running water, both inside and out. Rub dry with paper towel. Place chicken in a casserole with 1 cup water. Place the casserole in an oven preheated to 400 degrees for 15 minutes. Reduce heat to 350 degrees for 30 minutes. Remove casserole from oven. Open the lid and allow chicken to cool.

When cold, place chicken in a jar. Pour in the dry sherry. After 1 hour turn the chicken around and allow it to be immersed in the sherry for 2 days, turning it around every 12 hours.

When ready for use, chop chicken into 16 to 20 pieces. Serve as a starter, garnished with chopped parsley.

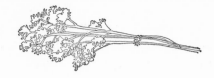

12

Duck

DUCKS ARE a very popular food in China, but not as widely or commonly used as chicken. One of the reasons for this is probably that the flavor of duck's meat is stronger and not quite as neutral as that of chicken and, therefore, cannot be combined with other foods as easily. For instance, there are very few diced (into cubes) duck meat dishes among Chinese recipes, while we have many of this type with chicken (see the chicken recipes). Ducks are usually cooked shredded, sliced, chopped, or as a whole. Many of the shredded and sliced duck dishes are prepared from cooked duck meat.

One of the best known of Chinese duck dishes is the "Peking Duck" which is a roast duck. This dish is by no means a "quick and easy" dish to cook, but it can be simplified. The following is a simplified version.

Peking Duck

1 duck, 3 to 3½ pounds

Dip duck in a pan of boiling water for 2 seconds. Remove and dry thoroughly. Hang it up in an airy place overnight. Place duck on a rack (with water-filled drip pan underneath to catch the drips) and insert in an oven preheated to 400 degrees. After the first 10 minutes reduce the heat to 375 degrees. Allow the duck to roast steadily for 1 hour without basting, turning it over twice. The duck skin will then be crisp and the meat well cooked. Allow 10 minutes extra roasting for every extra pound of duck.

Eating: One of the distinguishing things about Peking Duck is the way it is eaten. It is eaten wrapped in a pancake. In serving this dish you will have to prepare at least 1½ dozen very thin pancakes, as well as provide a couple of small dishes each of spring onions in 2-inch segments, sliced in half or quartered; and strips of cucumber cut to similar size. The duck meat and crispy skin, sliced while still very hot, are wrapped in a pancake by the diner and eaten together with a piece of spring onion and cucumber, and brushed with a liberal amount of Plum Sauce, or black currant jam and soy jam mixed; or use some soy sauce thickened simply by reducing to half by slowly heating and adding some sugar. Peking Duck is in fact a pancake dish (except that the pancake, often called a doily, is made with just flour and water and without the use of eggs).

Pancakes (or Doilies) for Duck

2 cups flour   2 tablespoons peanut oil,
1 cup boiling water   blended with 2 teaspoons
2 tablespoons sesame oil, or   peanut butter

Sift flour into a large basin and add boiling water slowly. Work with a wooden spoon into a warm dough. Knead 5 minutes and let stand for 10 minutes. Make dough into a long roll about 1½ to 2 inches in diameter. Cut off approximately ½-inch-thick pieces. With the aid of a knife, pat and flatten the pieces on a well-floured board into round thin dough-cakes of about 3-inch diameter. Brush the top of two dough-cakes liberally with sesame oil. Place one piece of "cake" on top of another, greased sides facing each other. Roll gently from center out into 6-inch-diameter double pancake, rolling on both sides. Repeat with remaining dough.

Heat ungreased heavy frying pan or griddle over medium heat. Place pancakes two at a time to heat for 3 to 3½ minutes on either side, or until some parts bubble and begin to turn brown. When slightly cooler pull each pancake apart into two (the greased sides should detach themselves quite easily). Fold each pancake across the center with the greased side inside.

Stack the pancakes on a heatproof dish, and place them in a steamer to steam vigorously for 10 minutes, then the pancakes or doilies should be ready for use. If no steamer is available place the heatproof dish with pancakes in a colander and set the latter over a pan of vigorously boiling water for 12 to 13 minutes. These pancakes can be stored in a refrigerator for several days, but will require 6 to 7 minutes of steaming again before using.

Aromatic and Crispy Duck

This is another dish where the duck meat is eaten wrapped in pancakes.

1 duck, 2 to 3 pounds	3 bags bouquet garni
4 cups Gunpowder Sauce	Oil for deep-frying
3 tablespoons sugar	

Give the duck a 3-minute dip in a pan of boiling water, and then place it to simmer for 30 minutes in the Gunpowder Sauce, to which the sugar and bouquet garni have been added.

Drain the duck thoroughly and heat the oil in the deep-fryer.

Lower the duck in a wire basket to deep-fry in the hot oil for 8 to 9 minutes.

When ready the duck is served and eaten in the same way as the Peking Duck, that is, slice the meat and skin off the duck and eat them wrapped in pancakes with spring onion and cucumber, brushed liberally with a sweet piquant sauce and thickened soy sauce (chutneys might be useful items to add).

Pan-roast Red-cooked Duck

1 3-pound duck	1 tablespoon chopped lemon
1 cup vegetable oil	rind
3 stalks spring onion (1-inch	4 tablespoons sherry
segments)	1 cup Gunpowder Sauce

Heat oil in a saucepan. Add duck to fry over high heat for 5 minutes turning it over all the time. Drain away oil. Add onion, lemon rind, sherry and Gunpowder Sauce. Continue to turn the duck over in the simmering liquid for 15 minutes. Transfer the duck and sauce to a casserole and insert in a pre-heated oven at 375 degrees to cook for 55 minutes, turning the bird over occasionally and adding a small amount of liquid (a couple of spoonfuls each of water, sherry and Gunpowder Sauce) if the pan gets too dry.

The duck can be served and eaten carved in the normal Western way, or chopped through bone into 16 to 20 pieces and reassembled on a dish and served in the Chinese way with two or three other dishes; or the meat can be used to cook into other duck dishes.

Orange Duck

½ roast duck
2 tablespoons vegetable oil
3 stalks spring onion (1-inch segments)
2 slices ginger root (optional but preferable)

3 tablespoons Gunpowder Sauce
2 teaspoons chutney
1 orange for garnish

For sauce:

Juice of 1 orange
1 tablespoon soy sauce
1 teaspoon sugar
2 tablespoons sherry

¾ tablespoon cornstarch blended in 3 tablespoons water

Squeeze juice from 1 orange and blend with other sauce ingredients into a consistent mixture.

Chop duck into bite-size pieces, 2 by 1½ inches. Stir-fry in oil with onion, ginger root and Gunpowder Sauce for 4 to 5 minutes over moderate heat. Reassemble and arrange neatly on a serving dish.

Add chutney to the pan, stir-fry in remaining oil for ¼ minute. Pour in the sauce mixture. As soon as the latter thickens pour it over the duck in the dish. Decorate the duck and dish with wedges and thin slices from the remaining orange.

Braised Duck with Mushrooms

6 large dried mushrooms
   (optional, but preferable)
6 large mushrooms
½ roast duck
2 tablespoons vegetable oil
1 tablespoon chopped spring
   onion
1 clove garlic, chopped
2 tablespoons Gunpowder
   Sauce
2 tablespoons sherry
¾ tablespoon cornstarch,
   blended in 4 tablespoons
   Broth

Soak dried mushrooms in ¼ cup warm water for half an hour (retain mushroom liquor). Cut mushrooms into quarters (remove stems). Chop duck into 2-by-1½-inch bite-size pieces.

Heat oil in a frying pan (with lid, or sautéing pan). Stir-fry onion and garlic and duck in it for 2 minutes. Add Gunpowder Sauce, sherry, mushroom liquor. Stir-fry for 2 minutes and push the duck to one side of the pan. Add the mushrooms to the center of pan. Mix them with the sauce and allow them to simmer gently under cover for 3 minutes. Open the lid, move the pieces of duck to a well-heated dish and arrange nicely. Pour the cornstarch mixture over the mushrooms. Stir them together over high heat. Ladle the mushrooms over the duck and pour the thickened sauce over them.

Braised Duck with Young Leeks

½ roast duck
4 tablespoons vegetable oil
1 clove garlic, chopped
2 stalks spring onion (1-inch segments)
2 cups young leeks (1-inch segments)

1 teaspoon salt
2 tablespoons sherry
3 tablespoons Broth
2 tablespoons Gunpowder Sauce

Chop duck through bone into bite-size pieces. Stir-fry them in two tablespoons oil with garlic and onion for 1 minute and push them to one side of a large frying pan.

Add remaining oil to the center of the dish. Add leeks and stir-fry them in the oil over high heat for 2 minutes. Sprinkle with salt. Pour in the sherry and Broth over the leeks. Stir-fry the leeks for another 1½ minutes. Remove leeks and arrange as bed on a well-heated dish.

Bring the duck back to the center of the pan. Pour the Gunpowder Sauce over it and stir-fry for 3 to 4 minutes over high heat, lay and arrange the duck on top of the leeks and serve.

Chopped Dry-fried Red-cooked Duck

1 duck, 2 to 3 pounds
4 tablespoons vegetable oil
1 clove garlic
1 tablespoon chopped onion

½ cup water
¼ cup Gunpowder Sauce
1 drop red food coloring

For final stir-frying:

2 tablespoons lard
2 tablespoons Gunpowder
  Sauce

2 tablespoons sherry
2 stalks spring onion (1-inch
  segments)

Chop duck through bone into 16 to 20 pieces. Heat oil in a
large saucepan. Add duck, garlic and onion. Stir-fry together
for 10 minutes. Drain away all fat. Pour in water and Gunpowder Sauce and add food coloring. Heat under cover for
10 minutes, turning the pieces of duck over a couple of times.

Turn heat up to the maximum, turning the duck over occasionally at first and rapidly as the sauce starts to dry. Just before the liquid is about to dry add the lard and other ingredients for the final stir-frying. Stir-fry until nearly all liquid
is gone. Arrange and serve on a well-heated dish.

Chopped Dry-fried Duck in
Wine Sediment Paste

Repeat the preceding recipe, using 4 to 6 tablespoons Wine
Sediment Paste instead of Gunpowder Sauce, in the final stir-
fry.

Shredded Duck with Stir-fried "Hot" Celery

½ roast duck
4 tablespoons vegetable oil
2 red chili peppers, seeded
  and shredded
2 cups celery, shredded into
  strips

1 teaspoon salt
2 tablespoons Gunpowder
  Sauce
1½ teaspoons sugar
4 tablespoons Broth
2 tablespoons sherry

Shred duck meat into thin strips.

Heat 2 tablespoons oil in a frying pan. Add shredded chili peppers. Stir-fry for ½ minute. Add celery. Sprinkle with salt and stir-fry over high heat for 3 minutes. Remove and put aside. Add the remaining oil to the pan. Add shredded duck's meat. Sprinkle with Gunpowder Sauce. Stir for 1 minute. Return chili pepper and celery to the pan. Sprinkle with sugar, Broth and sherry. Stir-fry over high heat for 3 minutes and serve.

Shredded Duck Stir-fried with Red Sweet Peppers and Bean Sprouts

Repeat the above recipe, using 1 cup spring onion (1-inch segments), 1 cup sweet pepper (sliced into thin strips), 1 cup bean sprouts. Fry the onion first with the chili pepper, then add sweet pepper and then bean sprouts — the procedure with the shredded duck and final stir-fry being the same as before.

Drunken Duck

Repeat the procedure under the recipe Drunken Chicken (see p. 123). Add 3 tablespoons chopped lemon rind to the mixture for the salting, and lengthen to 20 minutes the initial heating in the hot oven.

Excellent as a starter; or serve at cocktail parties with help of toothpick (after eliminating bone and cutting into smaller all-meat pieces).

Clear-simmered Duck with Onion and Spring Greens

1 duck, 4 to 4½ pounds	1 cup roast pork, chopped to
Boiling water	1-by-½-inch pieces, both
4 medium-size onions	lean and fat
4 hearts of spring greens	2 teaspoons salt
1 clove garlic, crushed	4 cups water

Dip duck in boiling water for 3 minutes and drain. Quarter the onions, trim the greens and cut the hearts into fours.

Stuff the cavity of the duck with onion and garlic and roast pork, adding 1 teaspoon salt. Sew or skewer to make secure. Place duck in a casserole and add 4 cups water. Place the casserole in a preheated oven at 400 degrees. After 15 minutes lower the temperature to 375 degrees.

After 1 hour, open the lid and skim away all excess fat. Insert the spring greens underneath the duck. Sprinkle with remaining salt. Return the casserole to the oven and continue to heat at 325 degrees for another hour. Serve in the casserole.

Clear-simmered Orange Duck with Onion, Ginger and Cabbage

1 duck, 4 to 4½ pounds	1 clove garlic, crushed
Boiling water	1 cup roast pork, chopped,
4 hearts of spring greens	lean and fat
1 large orange	2½ teaspoons salt
2 slices ginger root	1 pound cabbage or celery
2 medium-size onions	4 cups water

Repeat the preceding recipe, but this time substitute one large orange or two small ones for two of the onions. Prick a dozen holes in the orange before packing it into the cavity of the duck together with ginger root, onions, garlic and roast pork. Insert 1 pound of cabbage or celery under the duck during the second hour of simmering. Increase the salt added during the second stage of the cooking to 2½ teaspoons.

Wine-Simmered Duck

1 duck, 3 to 4 pounds	2 medium-size onions
1 large orange	4 cups Gunpowder Sauce
2 slices ginger root	2 bags bouquet garni
1 clove garlic, crushed	2 tablespoons sugar
1 cup chopped roast pork	1 bottle white wine

Clean the duck thoroughly and stuff it in the same manner as in Clear-simmered Orange Duck with Onion, Ginger and Cabbage. Bring the Gunpowder Sauce to boil in a saucepan with the added sugar and bouquet garni. Immerse the duck in the sauce to simmer gently for 1 hour. Drain (retain sauce for other uses) and transfer the duck to a casserole. Instead of water, pour in a bottle of dry white wine (or use beer). Close the casserole and insert it in an oven preheated to 350 degrees. Heat steadily at the temperature for 1 hour and serve in the casserole.

Long-simmered Duck with Mushrooms and Shredded Pork Toppings

Repeat recipe for Clear-simmered Duck with Onion and Spring Greens, but this time before stuffing the cavity of the duck stir-fry the stuffing in 2 tablespoons soy sauce and 1 teaspoon sugar in 1 tablespoon oil for 3 minutes.

For sauce:

4 tablespoons shredded pork in thin strips
4 tablespoons shredded mushrooms, or dried mushrooms soaked
4 tablespoons chopped spring onions

1 teaspoon chopped chili pepper
1 tablespoon vegetable oil
2 tablespoons soy sauce
1 teaspoon sugar
3 tablespoons sherry

When the duck is about ready stir-fry pork, mushrooms (or dried mushrooms soaked), spring onions and chili pepper in vegetable oil in small frying pan, adding soy sauce and sugar; and pouring over the duck, together with sherry, a minute before serving.

Eight Precious Duck

The so-called "Eight Precious Duck" is simply either a long-simmered or a long-steamed duck stuffed with eight items in varying amounts.

1 duck, 4 to 5 pounds   1 teaspoon salt
2 cups Broth

For stuffing:

Glutinous rice   Chinese sausages (substitute
Peas   salami)
Dried mushrooms, soaked and   Dates (remove stones)
  chopped to ¼-inch squares   Dried oysters or shrimps
Smoked ham   Water chestnuts

Mix stuffing ingredients which should weigh a total of 1½ to 2 pounds. When stuffed the bird should be sewn or skewered securely.

The duck is then placed at the center of a large casserole; 2 cups of Broth are poured over it and it is sprinkled with 1 teaspoon salt.

The casserole is then inserted in an oven preheated to 350 degrees for the first hour, and reduced to 325 degrees for the next 1½ hours.

When served the stuffing should be scooped out of the cavity and laid as a raised bed at the center of the serving dish, and the duck flattened out and laid spread-eagled on top of the stuffing.

13

Eggs

EGGS are very much an international food, and they occupy about the same place in Chinese cooking as in Western cooking. Since the majority of egg dishes can be prepared and cooked in a short time, they fall particularly in the sphere of "Quick and Easy Cooking."

Omelets

Basic Scrambled Omelet

We Chinese do not prepare our omelet in neat parceled fashion as you do in the West. Because we stir-fry the egg (in this case gently), the result is a cross between a scrambled egg and the Western idea of an omelet. Two ingredients we use with great success in our egg dishes — chopped spring onion and wine (sherry). The two generate a bouquet which endows a simple dish with near grandeur by its aromatic appeal.

1½ teaspoons salt	6 eggs
3 stalks spring onion (¼-inch segments)	4 tablespoons lard
	½ small glass of dry sherry

Add salt and spring onion to eggs and beat together for 10 seconds. Heat lard in a large frying pan over moderate heat. When it has all melted pour in the egg. Tilt the handle of the pan so that the egg will flow evenly over the pan. Leave to heat for 1 to 1½ minutes. Lift the sides of the egg so that the remaining liquid parts of the egg will flow under. When only about 10 to 15 percent of the eggs are still liquid, stir and turn them gently around with a spoon. Pour the sherry into the pan. Stir and turn once more. Dish out onto a well-heated platter and pour 2 tablespoons of good-quality soy sauce over it. Serve to be eaten immediately.

Triple-layer Scrambled Omelet with Shrimps

Repeat the preceding recipe using 9 eggs instead of 6, and in addition 1 cup fresh shrimp meat added to the eggs. Divide the stir-frying of the egg and shrimp into three sessions, each time using one-third of the mixture. After each frying, stir and turn once; when the eggs are about 85 percent hardened or set, sprinkle with sherry and pepper and transfer to a well-heated waiting dish. Repeat and place the next omelet on top of the first. Toward the end of the stir-frying of the last omelet pour over it an extra portion of sherry, so that when the last omelet is added on top of the first two the warm liquid will drip over the whole dish thus enhancing the bouquet. Pour two tablespoons good-quality soy sauce over the dish and bring quickly to the table to be consumed at once with rice.

Crab Scrambled Omelet

Crab omelet is seldom made in more than 1 layer, but a quantity of strong-tasting vegetable ingredients are usually incorporated into the initial frying.

1 teaspoon salt	3 tablespoons chopped spring
6 eggs	onion
1 small red sweet pepper	1 slice ginger root, shredded
4 tablespoons lard	(if available)
1 clove garlic, crushed and	1 cup crabmeat
chopped	3 tablespoons sherry

Add salt to eggs and beat for 15 seconds. Dice red pepper into ¾-inch squares.

Heat 2 tablespoons lard in a large frying pan. Add garlic, onion, ginger root and red pepper. Stir-fry for 1 minute. Add crabmeat, stir and spread out on the pan for 1 minute. Add remaining lard to the pan. When it has melted tilt the handle of the pan, so that the oil will run and cover the pan evenly. Now pour in the egg. Tilt the pan again, so that the egg will also run and cover the pan evenly. Heat for 1 minute or so. When only 10 to 15 percent of the eggs are still liquid give them a gentle stir and turn over. Pour the sherry over the pan. Give the omelet another gentle turn and scramble. Transfer the contents to a well-heated waiting dish to be served immediately.

Vegetarian Scrambled Omelet

Vegetarian Scrambled Omelet is a repeat of the preceding recipe, using 2 cups shredded vegetables (½ cup of each type, all shredded to thin strips) instead of crabmeat. Because of bulk, the vegetables may require 3 to 4 minutes of stir-frying together before they are added to the eggs. The most commonly used vegetables for the purpose are celery, bean sprouts, asparagus, carrots, sweet pepper, mushrooms, bamboo shoots. A small amount of sugar and soy sauce may be sprinkled on the shredded vegetables during the stir-frying. The vegetables are added to the eggs when the latter are 70 percent set.

Scrambled Omelet with
Sweet and Sour Sauce

Repeat recipe for Basic Scrambled Omelet, adding 4 tablespoons shredded ham to the beaten eggs. Heat half a cup of Sweet and Sour Sauce and pour it hot over the eggs when serving.

Egg-flower Meat

Egg-flower Meat, also known as the Pine-flower Meat is a typical Pekingese dish, where the eggs and shredded meat are stir-fried separately, and then brought together in a final assembly frying, when a small amount of sherry and an even smaller amount of sesame oil are added to seal the unity and contribute to the distinctive flavor of the dish.

¼ pound lean pork	2 tablespoons Broth
4 large mushrooms	1 teaspoon sugar
4 dried mushrooms, soaked for 30 minutes in warm water	½ teaspoon salt
	4 eggs
4 tablespoons lard	1 teaspoon sesame oil, or 2 teaspoons peanut butter diluted with 2 teaspoons vegetable oil
2 stalks spring onion (1-inch segments)	
1½ tablespoons soy sauce	½ glass sherry

Slice pork and mushrooms into thin strips.

Heat 2 tablespoons lard in a frying pan. When hot add onion, pork and mushrooms. Stir-fry over high heat for 2 minutes. Add soy sauce, Broth, sugar, and salt and stir-fry together for another minute. Remove pan from heat and keep warm.

Meanwhile, heat the remaining lard in another frying pan. When hot add the eggs. Heat until they have nearly hardened, stir and turn, and break up into small bright yellow pieces.

Return the pan containing pork and vegetables to the heat. Add sesame oil or peanut butter. When hot stir and scramble with meat vigorously for ½ minute. Now add the scrambled omelet from the other pan, pour half a glass of sherry over the contents. Stir-fry and scramble gently together for ½ minute and serve.

Soy-simmered Hard-boiled Eggs

Soy-simmered eggs are usually prepared when the eggs are cooked together with Red-cooked Pork during the last stages of the latter's cooking. The hard-boiled eggs are inserted into the meat-gravy for 20 to 30 minutes of slow simmering, during which the eggs are impregnated with the rich brown color of the gravy. These eggs are often served cold. When the meat is cold it is taken out, sliced into neat slices and served with the eggs, which are also sliced into thin slices. Arranged nicely on a dish with a pile of golden-crystallized meat jelly, the eggs and meat form an attractive hors d'oeuvre.

1 panful Red-cooked Pork with   6 hard-boiled eggs
   ample gravy   Few sprays of parsley
1 tablespoon gelatin

Heat Red-cooked Pork and add gelatin and hard-boiled eggs. See that the gelatin is completely dissolved and the eggs immersed in the gravy. Simmer gently for 25 minutes. Remove the eggs from the gravy and leave to cool. Transfer the pork and gravy to a large bowl and place in refrigerator.

When both the eggs and pork have cooled and the gravy has set into a jelly, remove or skim away the fat formed on top of the gravy. Dig out 5 or 6 spoonfuls of jelly and lay it down the middle of an oval dish. Slice the meat and arrange nicely in tile-piece fashion on top of the bed of jelly. Slice the eggs, each into about 10 thin slices, and arrange them in two lines beside the meat and gravy. Decorate with parsley and serve.

Oyster-stuffed Eggs

6 Soy-simmered Hard-boiled Eggs
2 tablespoons vegetable oil
2 tablespoons minced pork
1 clove garlic, chopped
2 tablespoons Wine Sediment Paste

12 oysters, shelled
2 teaspoons cornstarch, blended in 2 tablespoons Broth and 3 tablespoons Meat Gravy Sauce
1 tablespoon chopped chives

Cut each egg into halves. Scoop out the yolk and cut it neatly into halves. Cut a thin slice from the tip of each white half of egg so that they will be able to stand firmly.

Heat oil in a frying pan. Add pork and garlic and stir-fry over moderate heat for 1½ minutes. Add Wine Sediment Paste. Stir-fry together with pork until well blended. Pour in the oysters to stir-fry thoroughly with the pork and Wine Sediment Paste for 1½ minutes.

Stuff each half-egg with one oyster and some pork. Top with egg yolks. Heat cornstarch mixture in a small pan, and pour the thickened sauce over each of the stuffed half-eggs. Sprinkle with chopped chives and serve.

Pork-stuffed Eggs in Sweet and Sour Sauce

1 tablespoon vegetable oil
1 clove garlic, chopped
4 tablespoons minced pork
1 tablespoon soy sauce

1 tablespoon chopped chives
6 Soy-simmered Hard-boiled
  Eggs
½ cup Sweet and Sour Sauce

Heat oil in a small frying pan. Add garlic and pork and stir-fry together for 1½ minutes. Add soy sauce and chives and continue to stir-fry for another minute. Remove from heat.

Meanwhile cut each egg into halves and scoop out as in preceding recipe. Stuff each half with the fried pork filling and top it with the yolk. Arrange them neatly on a serving dish.

Heat the Sweet and Sour Sauce in a small pan and pour it over each of the stuffed eggs.

Steamed Eggs

Basic Steamed Eggs

This is a favorite dish for the aged and invalid.

3 eggs
1 teaspoon salt

2 cups Broth
½ tablespoon chopped chives

Beat eggs thoroughly with a fork for 15 seconds. Add with salt to the Broth. Blend them together to a very even consistency. Pour the mixture into a large deep-sided heatproof dish. Place in a steamer (or in a large boiler filled to a depth of 1 ½ inches with boiling water, the heatproof dish raised with a few eggcups or other platform), and steam vigorously for 10 minutes and gently for 10 minutes. Sprinkle with chopped chives and serve.

This dish, the consistency of which is more like a junket than a custard, is more interesting than it sounds and is excellent to go with rice. Its lightness contrasts well with the heavier dishes of a Chinese meal.

Fancy Steamed Eggs

Basic Steamed Eggs can be made more elaborate for those who are neither invalids nor aged by adding crabmeat or lobster meat to the eggs and Broth before steaming. As soon as top of the eggs becomes firm — which should be after 15 minutes' steaming — sprinkle gently on top some chopped smoked ham, a few well-chosen shrimps and a scatter of green peas and chives. Steam for a further 5 minutes. When seafoods are used, a tablespoon of sherry or white wine is sprinkled on before serving.

14

Fish

IN CHINESE COOKING we treat fish very much like meat. We prepare and cook it in very much the same manner; we red-cook, steam, long-simmer, braise and deep-fry it, but we do not stir-fry it in the brisk way we often stir-fry meat, as it will break into unsightly pieces if treated with the same vigor. When fish is quick-fried, it is usually fried statically or stirred around slowly in ample sauce.

The most important flavoring for fish comes from strong-flavored vegetables, such as ginger, garlic, onion, chives. A second line of flavoring comes from dried and salted vegetables, which, when soaked, often carry a much stronger flavor than when they were fresh. With these two types of flavoring acting in concert with meats and meat gravy and supported by soy sauce and other soybean products, together with wine, we Chinese are able to make our fish dishes as tasty and succulent as any of our meat dishes, if not more so.

The principal made-up sauces which are often called upon for fish cooking are Broth, Gunpowder Sauce, Meat Gravy Sauce and Wine Sediment Paste. (See Chapter 5.)

Since few fish can stand prolonged cooking (there are exceptions), the flavoring of fish is most often achieved through comparatively lengthy marinating and seasoning, followed by short sharp cooking — such as quick-steaming, deep-frying, quick-frying and braising. Although almost every kind of food can be red-cooked, fish is seldom red-cooked in the same way as meat, which is usually stewed for at least an hour or two. With fish red-cooking can perhaps more appropriately be called red-braising, with the process seldom lengthening to more than 10 or 15 minutes, generally less.

Red-cooked Fish (*whole*)

1 2-to-3-pound fish (carp, mullet, bream, bass, shad, salmon, etc.)	3 tablespoons sherry
	6 tablespoons Gunpowder Sauce
1½ teaspoons salt	4 slices bacon
½ tablespoon sugar	3 stalks spring onion (2-inch segments)
1 tablespoon capers, chopped	

Clean fish thoroughly and rub with salt. Mix sugar, capers, sherry with Gunpowder Sauce, and pour it over the fish, which is laid out on a deep-sided heatproof oval dish. Leave it to soak in the sauce for the next 15 minutes, turning it over every 5 minutes.

Cut two slices of bacon into ribbons, across lean and fat. When turning the fish over the last time, insert two slices of bacon underneath the fish. Drape the top of it with ribbons of bacon and segments of spring onion. Place the dish in a pre-heated oven at 425 degrees for 10 minutes. Baste the fish (use a few extra spoonfuls of Gunpowder Sauce if necessary) and reduce the temperature to 375 degrees for another 15 minutes of cooking in the oven. Serve in the original dish.

Red-cooked Fish (whole) Garnished with Ham and Vegetables

Presuming that there is no deep-fryer long enough to accom-modate the fish, it is best to finish its cooking in an oven.

1 3-pound fish	6 tablespoons vegetable oil
1½ teaspoons salt	4 slices bacon
2 tablespoons flour	

For sauce and garnish:

1 heart of spring greens	½ cup Meat Gravy Sauce
1 slice ham (about 1½ ounces)	2 tablespoons sherry
4 large mushrooms	1½ teaspoons sugar
2 stalks spring onion	1 tablespoon cornstarch
2 tablespoons vegetable oil	blended with 3 tablespoons Broth

Clean fish thoroughly. Rub with salt and flour. Heat oil in a roasting pan. Line it with slices of bacon. Lay the fish on top of the bacon to fry for 2 or 3 minutes over moderate heat. Turn the fish over and baste with hot oil with a large metal spoon for a further 2 or 3 minutes. Insert the roasting pan into an oven preheated to 450 degrees.

Meanwhile slice spring greens, ham and mushrooms into thin strips, and spring onion into 2-inch segments. Stir-fry them together in 2 tablespoons oil for 1½ minutes. Add the Meat Gravy Sauce and sherry and sugar. Allow the vegetables and ham to simmer in the sauce and gravy for 3 minutes. Add the cornstarch mixture to thicken.

When the fried fish has been in the hot oven for 10 minutes it should begin to be crispy. Transfer the fish with aid of fish slice and fork carefully onto a well-heated oval dish. Pour the sauce over the length of the fish and garnish with ham and vegetables in the sauce.

Red-cooked Fish Steaks

2 pounds fish steaks (cod, halibut, haddock)
1 teaspoon salt
1 egg
4 tablespoons flour
6 tablespoons water
4 tablespoons vegetable oil
2 stalks spring onion (1-inch segments)

1 clove garlic, crushed
6 tablespoons Gunpowder Sauce
4 tablespoons Meat Gravy Sauce
½ tablespoon cornstarch, blended in 2 tablespoons water

Cut fish into 2-inch squares. Mix salt, egg, flour, water into a light batter. Dip the pieces of fish in the batter.

Heat oil in a frying pan. Add onion and garlic, and stir-fry for 15 seconds. Push to one side. Add the pieces of fish one by one, laying them gently down into the oil in the pan, over moderate heat.

After 2 minutes' frying turn them over. After another minute's frying, pour the Gunpowder Sauce over them, allow them to simmer together for 3 minutes. Baste fish with the sauce in the pan for 1 minute. Transfer the fish steaks to a well-heated dish and keep hot in the oven. Meanwhile, add Meat Gravy Sauce and cornstarch mixture to the pan. Stir until the mixture thickens. Pour the mixture (sauce) over the fish and top it with the well-fried spring onion.

Plain Salted Double-fried Fish Steaks

2 fish steaks	2 stalks spring onion (1-inch
2 teaspoons salt	segments)
1 egg	1 clove garlic, crushed
4 tablespoons flour	2 slices ginger root or 1 tea-
6 tablespoons water	spoon dried ginger
Oil for deep-fry	Parsley
3 tablespoons vegetable oil	

Prepare fish and batter as in the preceding recipe, rubbing 2 teaspoons salt on the fish, leaving it to stand for half an hour before dipping in batter and cooking by deep-fry.

After deep-frying for 3 minutes, keep the pieces of fish hot. Meanwhile, fry onion and garlic in 3 tablespoons oil for 1 minute. Add the fish, ginger root or dried ginger to the oil;

turn over once and serve on a well-heated dish, piled up like a pyramid, topped with a few sprays of parsley.

Fish so cooked is best eaten dipped in tomato sauce, Tabasco or just plain.

Fish Steaks in Sweet and Sour Sauce

Use the same steaks as in the two previous recipes as well as the same batter. Either deep-fry them for 3 minutes and drain or pan-fry them (in 6 tablespoons vegetable oil for 2 minutes on either side).

Heat 1 cup Sweet and Sour Sauce and pour it over the fish steaks arranged on a well-heated dish.

Fish Steaks in Wine Sediment Paste

2 pounds fish steaks
4 tablespoons vegetable oil
2 stalks spring onion, chopped

1 clove garlic, chopped
6 tablespoons Wine Sediment
   Paste

For batter:

1 teaspoon salt
1 egg

4 tablespoons flour
4 tablespoons water

Cut fish into 2-inch squares. Mix batter ingredients into a thin batter. Dip fish in it.

Heat 3 tablespoons oil in a frying pan. Add chopped onion and garlic to fry for ½ minute and push to one side. Lay the pieces of fish onto the hot oil to fry for 1½ minutes on either side, basting as you go along. Add remaining oil and Wine Sediment Paste to the center of the pan. Stir until they are well-blended.

Turn the pieces of fish in the Wine Sediment Paste for a minute until each piece is well covered. Serve by arranging the pieces nicely on a well-heated dish, topped with the fried spring onion.

Fish Steaks in Sweet and Sour Sauce

Repeat preceding recipe, substituting Sweet and Sour Sauce for Wine Sediment Paste.

Sweet and Sour Carp

Although it might be best to deep-fry the whole fish, the cooking can be done partly in a hot oven as in recipe for Red-cooked Fish Garnished with Ham and Vegetables.

1 carp, 3 to 4 pounds
2 teaspoons salt
3 tablespoons flour
4 slices bacon
8 tablespoons vegetable oil

1 sweet pepper
1 tablespoon vegetable oil (for frying garnish)
1 cup Sweet and Sour Sauce

Clean fish thoroughly and rub with salt and flour both inside and out. Heat 8 tablespoons oil in a roasting pan. Line it with bacon and place the fish on top to heat over moderate heat for 4 to 5 minutes. Turn fish over and baste with hot oil for 3 to 4 minutes. Insert the roasting pan in an oven preheated to 450 degrees.

Meanwhile slice the pepper into strips and stir-fry in 1 tablespoon oil for 2 minutes. Add the Sweet and Sour Sauce to heat and simmer gently together.

When fish is ready in the oven (after 12 minutes), discard bacon and transfer fish to a well-heated oval dish. Pour the sauce over the length of the fish and garnish with sweet pepper.

Double-fried Eel

1 eel, 3 to 4 pounds
Oil for deep-fry
  2 tablespoons lard
  1 clove garlic, chopped
  2 stalks spring onion (1-inch
    segments)
½ tablespoon chopped lemon-
    rind shavings

2 stalks young leeks (1-inch
  segments)
1 teaspoon salt
2 tablespoons Meat Gravy
  Sauce
2 tablespoons Wine Sediment
  Paste
2 tablespoons sherry

Chop eel into 3-inch segments. Dip in boiling water for 1 minute. Drain and dry. Deep-fry in hot oil for 5 minutes. Scrape off all the meat without breaking it into too small pieces. Deep-fry the eel meat, using a wire basket, for another 2½ minutes in very hot oil. Drain thoroughly.

Meanwhile, heat lard in a frying pan. Add garlic, onion, lemon rind, leeks and salt. Stir-fry for 1 minute, add Meat Gravy Sauce, Wine Sediment Paste, and sherry. Stir-fry for half minute.

Add all the eel. Turn it in the sauce for 1 minute and serve. This is a favorite dish from Shanghai.

Long-simmered Fish in Vinegar Sauce

This is one of the few occasions where the fish is subjected to prolonged cooking.

6 small carp (or fat herrings or eel segments) about 2½ pounds
6 slices bacon
2 cloves garlic, crushed
2 onions, sliced
½ tablespoon sugar
1 red sweet pepper, sliced into strips
1 chili pepper, sliced into strips

2 tablespoons chopped lemon rind
6 tablespoons wine vinegar
6 tablespoons Gunpowder Sauce
1 cup red wine
2 tablespoons soy sauce
2 tablespoons sherry

Place the fish and bacon in alternate layers at the bottom of a casserole, starting with 3 slices of bacon. Scatter the garlic, onions, sugar, peppers and lemon rind evenly over the fish and pour in all the liquid ingredients. Add water until the fish is covered by a half-inch. Bring the contents to boil and insert the casserole into an oven preheated to 325 degrees for 1 hour under firm cover and reduce to 290 degrees for 2½ to 3 more hours.

By the end of the cooking even the bones of the fish should become soft enough to eat.

Clear-simmered Fish (whole)

1 fish, 2 to 3 pounds (sole, mullet, carp, bream, bass, etc.)
2 teaspoons salt
2 stalks young leeks

1 cup Broth
1½ teaspoons sugar
2 tablespoons sherry
1 clove garlic, chopped
1 teaspoon lemon juice

Clean and rub fish thoroughly with salt; leave to stand for 10 minutes. Cut leeks into 3-inch segments. Place the latter at the bottom of a roasting pan. Place the fish on top and pour in the Broth. Bring to boil quickly. Remove from heat, cover the top of the pan firmly with a sheet of tinfoil. Insert the pan in a preheated oven at 450 degrees for 10 minutes and reduce to 400 degrees for another 8 to 10 minutes. Transfer the fish to a deep-sided oval dish. Add sugar, sherry and garlic to the roasting pan. Stir over high heat for ½ minute. Pour the sauce over the fish and garnish it with young leeks which were cooked with it. Squeeze lemon juice over the fish. The liquid served with the fish can be drunk as a half soup, half gravy, which is excellent to go with rice.

Clear-simmered Fish (whole) with Shredded Pork and Mushroom Topping

Repeat the preceding recipe to the point where fish is transferred to the oval serving dish, using only 1½ teaspoons salt to rub the fish. Prepare the following topping in a separate pan:

For sauce:

1 cup shredded pork	½ teaspoon salt
½ cup shredded mushrooms	1 teaspoon sugar
2 stalks spring onion (1-inch segments)	Pinch of pepper
	1 slice ginger root, or ½ tablespoon chopped lemon rind
2 tablespoons oil	
3 tablespoons Meat Gravy Sauce	4 to 5 tablespoons fish stock

Quick-fry pork, mushrooms and spring onion in oil for 5 minutes; add remaining ingredients. Pour the resultant sauce over the fish.

Clear-simmered Fish (whole) with Hot Sauce

1 fish, 2 to 3 pounds	3 stalks young leeks
2 teaspoons salt	1 cup Broth

For sauce:

1 green pepper, sliced thin	4 tablespoons Meat Gravy Sauce
1 or 2 chili peppers, shredded	3 tablespoons fish stock
1 tablespoon chopped capers	lemon
½ teaspoon salt	

Repeat directions for Clear-simmered Fish (Whole) to the point when the fish is inserted into oven for 18 to 20 minutes' cooking.

In a separate pan, stir-fry green pepper and 1 or 2 red chili peppers (depending on how hot you want the dish) and capers. After 1 minute's stir-frying in oil, add salt, Meat

Gravy Sauce, stock from the fish dish, a squeeze of lemon, and continue to stir-fry over high heat for another minute. Pour the hot sauce over the fish and decorate with the two different-colored peppers.

Steamed Fish

Steam is readily available in the Chinese kitchen because of the cooking of rice. Steaming is often the method used for cooking fish, particularly as the time required for cooking a medium-sized fish (15 to 20 minutes for about 2 pounds) is often shorter than the time required to cook a large panful of rice (30 minutes for 5 to 6 pounds). For the best result fish should be salted, seasoned and marinated for 15 minutes or more and then subjected to a short sharp period of steaming.

Steamed Sole with Bacon and Mushroom Garnish

1 fat sole (about 1½ to 2 pounds	1 clove garlic, crushed and chopped
1 teaspoon salt	2 stalks spring onion
2 tablespoons Gunpowder Sauce	2 large mushrooms, dried if available
2 tablespoons chopped onion	2 slices bacon

Clean and rub fish with salt, Gunpowder Sauce and chopped onion and garlic. Leave to season for 15 minutes.

Cut spring onion into 2-inch segments, and mushrooms into similar strips (if dried mushrooms, slice after 20 minutes' soaking in hot water), slice bacon across lean and fat into strips.

Place fish in an oval or oblong heatproof dish. Garnish with spring onion, mushrooms and bacon. Pour the marinade over the length of the fish. Place the fish in a steamer for 15 to 16 minutes' vigorous steaming. Serve in the original dish.

Steamed Fish (sole, mullet, bream, etc.) with Shredded Pork Garnish and Hot Sauce

Proceed according to the preceding recipe, but do not garnish the fish before steaming. Insert the fish into the steamer for 15 or 20 minutes' steaming (20 minutes if over $2\frac{1}{2}$ pounds) directly after seasoning.

For sauce:

½ cup shredded pork	½ tablespoon chopped lemon-
1 shredded sweet pepper	rind shavings
1 tablespoon chopped capers	1 tablespoon tomato sauce
1½ teaspoons Tabasco	1 tablespoon soy sauce
4 tablespoons Meat Gravy	2 tablespoons sherry
Sauce	2 tablespoons vegetable oil

Meanwhile, stir-fry shredded pork, sweet pepper, capers, Tabasco, Meat Gravy Sauce, chopped lemon-rind shavings, tomato sauce, soy sauce, sherry, in vegetable oil for 4 minutes over high heat. Pour the sauce over the length of the fish, garnishing with pork and pepper, as it is taken out from the steamer. Serve in the original dish.

Casserole of Fish Steaks in Tomato Sauce

2 pounds fish steaks	6 medium-size tomatoes
1½ teaspoons salt	4 tablespoons Meat Gravy
1 tablespoon flour	Sauce
3 tablespoons vegetable oil	2 tablespoons sherry
1 onion, chopped	¾ tablespoon cornstarch,
1 clove garlic, chopped	blended in 6 tablespoons
1 tablespoon chopped capers	Broth

Cut fish into 2-inch-square pieces. Rub with salt and flour. Heat oil in casserole. Add onion, garlic, capers. Stir-fry for ½ minute. Add fish. Fry on either side for 1 minute, remove with perforated spoon and put aside.

Meanwhile, skin the tomatoes (by dipping into boiling water). Cut each into halves and add to the casserole to fry in the remaining oil, over high heat for 1 minute. Add the Meat Gravy Sauce.

Stir-fry for 1 minute. Add sherry and the cornstarch mixture. Stir until the sauce is smooth and thickened. Place the pieces of fish spread out in the sauce. Scoop and pour some sauce over each piece of fish. Close the casserole with a lid, and allow it to simmer over low heat for 4 to 5 minutes; serve in the casserole.

Casserole of Fish Steaks with Mushrooms

6 large dried mushrooms	6 large mushrooms
2 pounds fish steaks	Oil for frying
1½ teaspoons salt	½ cup Broth, blended with 3
1 tablespoon flour	teaspoons cornstarch
3 tablespoons vegetable oil	2 tablespoons sherry
1 onion, chopped	1 teaspoons salt
1 clove garlic, chopped	½ cup mushroom liquid
1 tablespoon chopped capers	

Soak dried mushrooms in ¾ cup hot water for 30 minutes. Retain the liquor.

Repeat directions for preparing fish in the preceding recipe to the point where the fish is removed after the initial frying.

Remove the stems from both types of mushrooms and cut into halves. Fry them in oil over moderate heat for 1½ minutes. Pour in Broth blended with cornstarch, sherry, salt and ½ cup mushroom liquor. Stir until the liquid reboils and thickens. Return the fish to the casserole. Spread it out, and spoon some mushrooms and soup over each piece of fish. Close the lid of the casserole and cook over low heat for 5 minutes; serve in the casserole.

Casserole of Fish Steaks with Watercress, Parsley, Pickles and Salted Vegetables

2 pounds fish steaks	1 onion, chopped
1½ teaspoons salt	1 clove garlic, chopped
1 tablespoon flour	1 tablespoon chopped capers
3 tablespoons vegetable oil	

For sauce:

1 tablespoon capers, chopped

2 tablespoons chopped
chutney

2 tablespoons sliced gherkins

3 tablespoons parsley,
chopped coarsely

3 tablespoons watercress

Oil for frying

1 cup Broth

4 tablespoons sherry

1 tablespoon soy sauce

½ teaspoon salt

Repeat directions for preparing fish in Casserole of Fish Steaks
in Tomato Sauce to the point where the fish is removed after
the initial frying.

Add capers, chutney, gherkins, parsley and watercress to
stir-fry for 1 minute in oil. Pour in Broth and sherry; add soy
sauce, salt. Return fish to the casserole. Spread the pieces out.
Heat until the liquid boils. Close the lid, simmer for 5 minutes over low heat and serve in the casserole.

Stuffed Fish Simmered in Wine

1 large fish, 3 to 4 pounds
(carp, mullet, bass, salmon)

2 teaspoons salt

3 tablespoons flour

½ pound (approximately 1
cup) roast pork (Chinese or
Western), cut into 1-by-½-
inch pieces

2 cloves garlic, crushed

6 stalks spring onion (1-inch
segments)

½ cup vegetable oil for
semideep-fry

1½ cups Broth

1½ cups white wine (dry)

4 tablespoons Gunpowder
Sauce

2 teaspoons sugar

Clean fish and rub with salt and flour. Stuff cavity with pork, garlic and spring onion. Skewer or sew to secure.

Heat oil in an oval casserole. When very hot lower fish to fry in it for 5 minutes. Baste continually, turning the fish over once. Drain away all the oil.

Pour into the casserole Broth, wine and Gunpowder Sauce and sugar. Bring to gentle boil. Close the lid of the casserole and simmer for ½ hour. Serve in the casserole.

Stuffed Fish Simmered in Wine and Vinegar Sauce

2 fish, 1 to 2 pounds each (small carp, mullet, or large herring)
1½ teaspoons salt
3 tablespoons flour
4 stalks spring onion (1-inch segments)
2 cloves garlic, crushed
4 tablespoons smoked haddock

4 tablespoons mussels (fresh) or oysters
4 tablespoons smoked ham
1 cup oil for semideep-fry
2 stalks young leeks (1-inch segments)
1 cup Broth
1 cup dry white wine
4 tablespoons wine vinegar
1 tablespoon soy sauce

Clean and rub fish, inside and out, with salt and flour. Divide the stuffings (onion, garlic, haddock, mussels, ham) in two, and stuff the cavities of the fish. Sew or skewer to secure.

Heat oil in a casserole. Lower the fish to fry in the oil over moderate heat for 4 to 5 minutes. Pour and drain away all the oil. Place the leeks underneath the fish. Pour in the Broth, wine, vinegar and soy sauce. Bring to boil and simmer gently for 30 minutes. Serve in the casserole.

Four Treasure Stuffed Simmered Fish

Repeat the preceding recipe, stuffing the fishes with 4 table-spoons diced cooked chicken, 4 tablespoons mushrooms, 4 tablespoons diced ham, 6 tablespoons cooked rice and without the use of vinegar in the simmering.

Quick-fried Sliced Fish

Sliced fish differs from fish steaks in that it is always very thinly sliced (about ⅛ inch thick) which makes it possible to cook it in an instant. It is almost always wet quick-fried, that is quick-fried in sauce. The operation is a much more delicate one than the cooking of larger pieces of fish in that, being so thin, they break up into unsightly pieces very easily. There-fore, only very firm and fresh fish can be used for this type of cooking.

Sliced Fish Quick-fried in Wine Sauce

1¼ pounds very fresh filleted
    fish (sole, halibut, carp,
    cod)
1 teaspoon salt
1 egg white
2 tablespoons cornstarch
4 tablespoons vegetable oil
1 slice ginger root

1 tablespoon finely chopped
    onion
4 tablespoons dry white
    wine
1 tablespoon cornstarch,
    blended in 6 tablespoons
    Broth
1½ teaspoons sugar

Cut fish with sharp knife into thin slices approximately 2 inches by 1 inch. Rub with salt. Beat egg white for 30 seconds with a rotary beater. Dip fish in the egg white and dust lightly with cornstarch.

Heat oil in a frying pan over moderate heat. Add ginger root and onion to fry in it for half a minute. Lay the pieces of sliced fish gently in the sizzling oil to fry for ¾ minute on either side. Remove with help of fish slice and keep hot.

Drain away any excess of oil in the pan. Add wine, cornstarch mixture, and sugar. Stir until the sauce thickens. Return the pieces of sliced fish to the pan. Spread them out and turn them in the simmering sauce for ¾ minute. Serve on a well-heated dish; to be eaten immediately.

Sliced Fish Quick-fried in Sweet and Sour Sauce

Repeat the preceding recipe, substituting ½ cup Sweet and Sour Sauce for wine and cornstarch mixture, adding 1 tablespoon sweet pickles to the frying just before adding the Sweet and Sour Sauce, and 2 tablespoons sherry after the fish has been introduced to the sauce for the final assembly frying.

Sliced Fish Quick-fried in Meat Gravy Sauce

Repeat recipe for Sliced Fish Quick-fried in Wine Sauce, substituting 6 tablespoons Meat Gravy Sauce and 1 tablespoon sherry for white wine and reducing cornstarch mixture to ½ tablespoon cornstarch blended in 2 tablespoons cold Broth in the final assembly frying.

Sliced Fish Quick-fried in Wine Sediment Paste

Repeat recipe for Sliced Fish Quick-fried in Wine Sauce, substituting 6 tablespoons Wine Sediment Paste for white wine and using ½ tablespoon cornstarch blended with 2 tablespoons Broth in the final assembly frying.

Toasted Fish

2 eggs	2 cups bread crumbs
½ teaspoon salt	Oil for deep-fry
4 slices bread	2 tablespoons coarsely
1 pound filleted fish	chopped parsley

Beat eggs and salt with a rotary whisk for 15 seconds. Cut

away the crust from the bread, and cut each slice into six. Slice fish to approximately the same size as the bread. Spread half the bread crumbs on a large plate or tray.

Dip each piece of fish and bread quickly in the beaten egg to take on a light coating. Place the fish on top of the bread, pressing them lightly together; and place the miniature open sandwich on the bread crumbs spread out on the tray. Sprinkle each piece heavily with additional bread crumbs, both from the reserved half and from the tray. Proceed until all the pieces of fish and bread are used up and formed into bread-crumbed canapés.

Heat oil in a deep-fryer. When very hot place six canapés in a wire basket and deep-fry six at a time for approximately 2½ minutes. You will note that as soon as the canapé is sunk in the hot oil it becomes one firm piece. When all the pieces have been fried, arrange them nicely on a well-heated serving dish, place a pinch of parsley on top of each piece and serve. An appealing and useful dish, particularly at a cocktail party.

15

Shellfish

As CROSS-COOKING and cross-blending of flavors are very much in the tradition of Chinese cooking, shellfish are used as often for flavoring as for food. In this section we shall, however, deal with them mainly as food — that is, when they are the principal material in a given dish, or at least provide its principal flavor.

Abalone

This rubbery-textured shellfish is used much more often as a flavorer than as food, but there are a number of abalone dishes. Like most seafoods, abalone requires very little cooking.

Abalone Quick-fried with Mushrooms and Broccoli

1 10-ounce can abalone
  (reserve liquid)
½ tablespoon cornstarch,
  blended in 4 tablespoons
  abalone liquid
6 large dried mushrooms
6 large mushrooms
1 cup broccoli, chopped to
  inch-long pieces

2 tablespoons vegetable oil
1 tablespoon chopped onion
1 clove garlic, chopped
4 tablespoons Meat Gravy
  Sauce
1 tablespoon soy sauce
1 tablespoon sherry

Slice the abalone into approximately 2-by-1-inch pieces. Blend 4 tablespoons abalone liquid with cornstarch. Soak dried mushrooms in ½ cup hot water for 20 minutes (retain liquor). Destem both types of mushroom and cut into quarters. Parboil broccoli for 5 minutes.

Heat oil in a frying pan. When hot add onion and garlic. Stir-fry over moderate heat for ½ minute. Add broccoli and mushrooms and stir-fry together for 1½ minutes. Add sliced abalone and Meat Gravy Sauce and stir-fry for a further minute. Finally, add abalone liquid (blended with cornstarch), soy sauce, sherry and 3 tablespoons mushroom liquor. Stir until sauce thickens. Serve on a well-heated dish.

Abalone Quick-fried with Sliced Chicken and Mushrooms

Repeat the preceding recipe, substituting sliced chicken (one breast of chicken sliced to the same size as the abalone) for broccoli, but add the chicken together with mushrooms immediately when the garlic and onion have been fried for ½ minute. Stir-fry together for 1½ minutes before adding the abalone and Meat Gravy Sauce for ½ minute's stir-fry. A teaspoon of Tabasco may be introduced here before adding the blended cornstarch mixture for the final stir-fry together.

Abalone with Chopped Red-cooked Pork

1 can abalone (about 10   2 tablespoons sherry
  ounces)   2 pounds Red-cooked Pork
1 tablespoon cornstarch   with gravy

Slice abalone into 2-by-1-inch slices. Retain liquid and blend 6 tablespoons with 1 tablespoon cornstarch.

Heat pork and gravy together with abalone in a saucepan (pork and abalone interleaving). When hot add the cornstarch mixture and sherry. Simmer together for 3 minutes and serve in a bowl or deep-sided dish.

Clams

Clams Simmered in Clear Consommé

8 clams
1 breast of chicken
1 cup water
1 teaspoon salt

1 cup Broth
2 tablespoons sherry
1 tablespoon chives, chopped

Shell clams. Remove impurities and intestines, using only the white meat of the clams. Slice each into 2 or 3 slices. Cut chicken into similar sizes.

Heat water in a frying pan. Add salt and chicken. Simmer gently for 3 minutes. Skim away any impurities, pour away half the water. Add Broth and sherry and clams. Simmer them together for 2½ minutes. Sprinkle with chopped chives and serve.

(Clams cooked lightly in this manner should be eaten dipped in good-quality soy sauce, soy-Tabasco dip, soy-vinegar dip or soy-sherry dip, and tomato sauce, which should all be placed in sauce dishes at strategic points on the dining table.)

Stuffed Deep-Fried Clams

6 clams	1 tablespoon flour
½ cup lean and fat pork	1 clove garlic, crushed and
1 egg	chopped
1 teaspoon salt	A dash of cinnamon
1 tablespoon finely chopped	Oil for deep-fry
onion	Parsley

Clean and remove unwanted parts from the clam as in the previous recipe. Reserve shells. Poach the clam meat in boiling water to simmer for 1½ minutes. Drain and reduce in a mincer to a fine mince. Simultaneously boil pork vigorously for 5 minutes and reduce to similar fine-grain mince. Mix the two minces together with all the other ingredients, including egg and flour, into a consistent paste. Stuff the paste into the 12 half-shells.

Heat the oil in the deep-fryer to a high temperature. Lower 6 stuffed shells at a time to deep-fry for 3½ to 4 minutes. Keep very hot. Repeat with remaining 6 stuffed shells. When all the 12 shells are ready, arrange on a heat-proof dish. Decorate with sprigs of parsley, and serve. The dish should be eaten accompanied by the same dips as in the previous recipe.

Crabs

An enormous quantity of crabs is eaten in China. They are either cooked in their shells or the crabmeat is extracted and cooked with other materials.

Quick-fried Crabs in Egg Sauce

2 large crabs
3 tablespoons vegetable oil
2 tablespoons chopped
  onions
2 cloves garlic, chopped

1 tablespoon chopped capers
1½ teaspoons salt
3 teaspoons vinegar
1 tablespoon sherry

For Egg Sauce:

2 egg yolks
4 tablespoons water
½ cup Broth

1 tablespoon cornstarch
½ teaspoon salt

Remove top shells of crabs. Chop body into 6 pieces, each with leg or claw attached. Chop shell into two, and crack claws with back of chopper.

Beat egg yolk and water together for 15 seconds. Blend cornstarch with Broth and salt. Heat the latter mixture in a small pan until the sauce is smooth and thickens. Stream in the egg yolk mixture slowly in a very thin stream, forming a cloud effect in the sauce. Stir and remove from heat.

Heat oil in a large frying pan. Add onion, garlic and capers, to stir-fry together for half a minute. Add the chopped crabs, sprinkle with salt to stir-fry over high heat for 2½ minutes. Stream in the egg sauce over the crab, especially over the meatier parts. Add vinegar and sherry. Lower the heat, place the lid over the pan and allow contents to simmer for 2 or 3 minutes. Serve immediately. (The great pleasure and taste in eating this dish lies in sucking the meat and sauce out of the body of the crab, holding on to its leg or claw. The latter should be cracked open and eaten last.)

The only traditional sauce used on the table for dipping is ginger and vinegar mix (1 tablespoon shredded ginger root mixed with 3 to 4 tablespoons vinegar; or 1 tablespoon chopped dried ginger soaked in 4 tablespoons vinegar).

Deep-fried Crabs

2 to 3 crabs (medium to large)   Oil for deep-fry

For batter:

1 egg
3 tablespoons flour
4 tablespoons water
1 teaspoon salt

2 cloves garlic, crushed and
   chopped
1 tablespoon chopped spring
   onion

Steam the crabs vigorously for 5 minutes by placing them in a heatproof basin, and lowering the latter into a large boiler or saucepan with boiling water 1½ inches deep. Close the lid and keep water at a rolling boil for 5 to 6 minutes.

Remove the top shells from the crabs, and chop body into 4 to 6 pieces, each piece with a leg or claw attached. Crack the latter slightly with a rolling pin or back of chopper.

Mix the ingredients for the batter together into a smooth batter. Dip the meat end of the pieces of crab in the batter. Heat the oil in the deep-fryer and deep-fry the pieces of crab in two lots (including shell) for 3½ to 4 minutes each. Serve by arranging the pieces and shells nicely on a well-heated dish.

Deep-fried Crabs can be eaten with fingers, dipping the legs and claws in ginger-vinegar dip, or any of the dips used in recipe for Clams Simmered in Clear Consommé.

Grilled Crab

Crabs can also be grilled or barbecued. Since in the modern kitchen it is easier to grill than barbecue, this is the method which can be recommended. In this case, the crab, dipped in batter, should be placed under the grill at high heat for 3 minutes on each side. If crabs have been steamed reduced grilling time to 1½ minutes on each side. For refinement, the pieces of crab can be lightly brushed with onion-impregnated oil (simmer 2 tablespons onion in 3 tablespoons oil for 3 minutes) before dipping in batter.

Quick-fried Crabmeat with Pork and Eggs

2 cups crabmeat
4 eggs
2 stalks spring onion
2 tablespoons lard
1 cup minced pork
1 clove garlic, chopped

1 tablespoon chopped onion
1 teaspoon salt
1 tablespoon soy sauce
2 tablespoons sherry
¾ teaspoon sugar

Shred crabmeat, beat eggs lightly. Chop spring onion into 1-inch segments. Heat lard in a frying pan. Add pork, garlic and chopped onion. Sprinkle with salt. Stir-fry together over high heat for 3 minutes. Add crabmeat. Sprinkle with soy sauce, half the sherry and sugar, and stir-fry together for 1 minute. Add spring onion and pour in the eggs. As soon as the latter begin to set sprinkle with remaining sherry. Stir and scramble the egg and crab together lightly and serve.

Quick-fried Crabmeat with Pork and Vegetables

Crabmeat can be cooked with many vegetables effectively by repeating the preceding recipe, substituting a vegetable (chopped to approximately inch-square pieces) for eggs. Fry a couple of minutes longer, and use an extra tablespoon of lard just before the vegetables (which have had 3 minutes of parboiling) are added to the pan. An extra half-teaspoon salt and 2 to 3 tablespoons Broth may be added for the final assembly frying. This applies to vegetables like cauliflower, broccoli, celery or Chinese celery cabbage, but with vegetables like spinach the parboiling is unnecessary.

Lobsters

Lobsters are very similar to crab for the purposes of Chinese cooking. They can be cooked in the majority of ways that crabs are cooked (the difference being only one of shape). In China lobsters are treated with a little more respect than crabs because of their comparative rarity. They are called the "Dragon Shrimps."

Lobster and Pork in Egg Sauce

1 lobster, 1½ to 2 pounds
3 tablespoons vegetable oil
1 clove garlic, chopped
2 tablespoons chopped spring
 onion
½ cup lean pork, minced
1 teaspoon salt

2 tablespoons soy sauce
2 slices chopped ginger root
 (preferable, if available,
 otherwise use 1 tablespoon
 chopped lemon-rind
 shavings)

For the Egg Sauce:

2 eggs
½ teaspoon salt
¼ cup water
1 tablespoon cornstarch

½ cup Broth
3 tablespoons sherry
1 teaspoon sugar

After cleaning thoroughly cut lobster lengthwise with sharp knife or chopper, and then cut into segments of about 1½ inches. Crack the claws.

Heat oil in a heavy saucepan. Add garlic and onion to stir-fry over high heat for half a minute. Add pork and stir-fry for 3 minutes. Add the lobster segments. Sprinkle with salt and continue to stir-fry for 1½ minutes. Add soy sauce and ginger root. Meanwhile beat eggs and blend with salt and water. Blend cornstarch with cold Broth, sherry and sugar. Pour the cornstarch mixture into the pan. Stir the lobster in the sauce. Lower the heat slightly and stream in the egg-water mixture in a thin stream, streaming it in evenly over lobster segments and sauce. Stir the contents of the pan around once. Close the lid of the pan, allow the contents to simmer for 2 minutes and serve in a well-heated deep-sided dish.

Baked Lobster

1 lobster, 1½ to 2 pounds	4 tablespoons Broth
1 egg	1 tablespoon soy sauce
¼ cup minced pork	2 tablespoons sherry
1 tablespoon flour	2 tablespoons vegetable oil
2 tablespoons chopped onion	1 tablespoon chopped parsley
1 clove garlic, chopped	
2 teaspoons chopped lemon-rind shavings	

Prepare lobster as in the preceding recipe. Place the segments meat-side up on a heatproof dish. Beat egg lightly. Combine with pork, flour and all the other ingredients. Mix and beat them together for 15 seconds. Spread the mixture thickly over each open meaty segment of lobster. Place the dish in an oven preheated at 450 degrees for 13 to 15 minutes. Sprinkle with chopped parsley and serve.

Shrimps, Prawns and Scallops

In China these seafoods or fresh-water products are, as often as not, used as flavorers — particularly in their dried state — rather than as food. When cooked fresh, since they never require prolonged cooking, they are mostly stir-fried for a minute or two, either by themselves or in combination, which enables them to produce innumerable varieties of dishes. Prawn, shrimp and scallop dishes are very convenient as, apart from being quick to cook, they require very little chopping and cutting. With scallops, after shelling, the meat is often cut into two or three slices before cooking. Shrimps and prawns are often cooked in their shells after thorough washing and removal of the gritty parts and impurities. There is a thought in China that shellfish cooked in their shells are more tasty. Since they are extremely tasty in any case, so long as they are fresh, we do not have to be biased in favor of cooking them in their shells. Particularly with Westerners, who are not trained or adept in extracting bones and shells from their mouths, it is best to conceive of dishes where the shellfish are already shelled (in any case these foods are often bought, frozen or fresh, ready shelled). However, we shall start with one dish of shrimps (or prawns), which are cooked in their shells.

Dry-fried Shrimps (or Giant Prawns)

6 to 8 large shrimps or prawns	2 tablespoons vegetable oil
2 stalks spring onion	1 tablespoon chopped onion
2 tablespoons Broth	1 clove garlic, chopped
1 tablespoon soy sauce	½ teaspoon salt
1 tablespoon sherry	1 tablespoon lard
1 teaspoon sugar	

Clean shrimps thoroughly, remove dark and gritty parts. Drain and dry. Chop spring onion into 1-inch segments. Mix latter in a bowl with Broth, soy sauce, sherry and sugar.

Heat oil in frying pan. Add onion and garlic to stir-fry for ¼ minute over high heat. Add shrimps, sprinkle with salt and stir-fry for 1¼ minutes. Pour in the Broth–soy sauce mixture. Stir the shrimps in the sauce until the latter dries, which it should do in about 1 or 2 minutes. Add lard and chopped spring onion. Stir-fry for half a minute. Serve on a well-heated dish.

The normal way we Chinese eat this type of shrimp is to put a whole or half shrimp in the mouth, and by gradually biting and squeezing the end nearest our front teeth, we squeeze the meat out, like toothpaste from the tube, and this is accompanied by a sucking action, which also helps in the extraction; while all the time the near-dried sauce is imparting a sharp savoriness to the mouth as well as to the meat of the shrimp. This is a classical banquet dish.

Quick-fried Scallops with Wine Sediment Paste

2 pounds scallops
2 tablespoons lard
2 teaspoons chopped lemon rind
1 clove garlic, chopped
1 teaspoon salt
1 tablespoon chopped spring onion
2 tablespoons Broth
3 tablespoons Wine Sediment Paste

Wash and shell scallops, removing tough root muscles, and slice each scallop into 3 or 4 pieces.

Heat lard in a frying pan over high heat. Add lemon rind, garlic and salt. Stir-fry for ¼ minute, add spring onion and scallop. Continue to stir-fry for 1½ minutes. Add Broth and Wine Sediment Paste; stir-fry for a further minute and serve on a well-heated dish.

Quick-fried Shrimps with Wine
Sediment Paste

Repeat the preceding recipe, substituting 1 pound shrimp meat
for scallops.

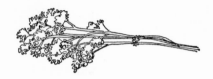

Quick-fried Shrimps (or Scallops) with
Mushrooms in Meat Gravy Sauce

1 teaspoon sugar
1 tablespoon sherry
¾ tablespoon cornstarch,
   blended in 2 tablespoons
   water
4 tablespoons mushroom
   liquor
6 large mushrooms,
   destemmed
6 large dried mushrooms,
   soaked in 1 cup hot water
   for 20 minutes, destemmed

3 tablespoons lard
1 tablespoon chopped onion
1 clove garlic, chopped
1 teaspoon chopped lemon
   rind
½ teaspoon salt
1 pound shrimp or scallop
   meat
4 tablespoons Meat Gravy
   Sauce

Mix sugar, sherry, cornstarch mixture, half of mushroom liquor
in a bowl. Cut each piece of mushroom into quarters.

Heat lard in a frying pan. Add onion, garlic, lemon rind

and salt, to stir-fry for ½ minute. Add mushrooms to fry together for 1 minute. Add the shrimps or scallops to stir and fry together for ½ minute. Pour in the Meat Gravy Sauce, mushroom-liquor and cornstarch mixture, continue to stir-fry together for 2½ minutes and serve.

Quick-fried Shrimps (or Giant Prawns) with Tomatoes

Repeat the recipe for Dry-fried Shrimps (or Giant Prawns). Skin 4 medium-size tomatoes, and add them to the pan, after the shrimps have been initially fried for ½ minute. Stir-fry them together for 1 minute over high heat, before adding the Broth-soy sauce mixture. Continue to stir-fry for 1 more minute. Here 1 tablespoon tomato sauce may be added with 1 teaspoon Tabasco. Serve on a well-heated dish.

Quick-fried "Crystal Shrimps"

2 cups shrimp meat, frozen or fresh
1 teaspoon salt
2 tablespoons sherry
2 tablespoons vegetable oil
1 tablespoon onion, finely chopped
1 clove garlic, crushed and chopped

2 tablespoons Broth
½ tablespoon cornstarch, blended in 2 tablespoons water and 1 tablespoon sherry
½ tablespoon chopped chives

Sprinkle shrimps (should be thawed if frozen) with salt and

sherry. Leave to soak for 10 minutes and drain away any liquid.

Heat oil in a frying pan. Add onion and garlic and stir-fry over moderate heat for 1 minute. Add the shrimps, spread them out and stir-fry gently for 1½ minutes. Pour in the Broth. Mix and stir-fry together with shrimps for half a minute. Pour in the cornstarch-water-sherry mixture. Stir until the sauce thickens and is well mixed with the shrimps. Sprinkle with chives, dish out onto a well-heated platter and serve; to be eaten immediately.

Quick-fried Shrimps with Fu Yung Sauce

1 cup shrimp meat, thawed if frozen
1 teaspoon salt
2 tablespoons sherry
2 tablespoons vegetable oil
1 tablespoon onion, finely chopped

1 clove garlic, finely chopped
1½ tablespoons lard
1 cup diced cucumber, diced to ¼-inch cubes
2 tablespoons Broth
6 tablespoons Fu Yung Sauce

Sprinkle shrimps with salt and sherry; leave to season for 10 minutes. Drain away liquid.

Heat oil in a frying pan. Add onion and garlic to stir-fry for ½ minute. Add shrimps and stir-fry for 1 minute. Add lard and cucumber and continue to stir-fry for 1½ minutes. Add Broth followed by Fu Yung Sauce. Mix and stir together for 1 minute and serve.

Stir-fried "Phoenix" and "Dragon"

1 cup shrimp meat
1 teaspoon salt
2 tablespoons sherry
1 breast of chicken
1 3-inch section cucumber,
  scraped but not peeled
2 tablespoons vegetable oil
1 tablespoon onion, finely
  chopped

1 clove garlic, crushed and
  chopped
2 tablespoons lard
½ cup button mushrooms
3 tablespoons Wine Sediment
  Paste
1 teaspoon sugar
1 tablespoon soy sauce

Sprinkle shrimps with salt and sherry; leave for 10 minutes and drain away liquid. Dice chicken and cucumber into ¼-inch cubes.

Heat oil in a frying pan. Add onion and garlic to stir-fry for 1 minute. Add shrimps and chicken. Stir-fry them together for 2 minutes. Remove with perforated spoon and put aside.

Add lard to the pan. When it has melted, add diced cucumber and mushrooms. Stir-fry them together for 1 minute. Push them to the sides of the pan. Add Wine Sediment Paste to the center of the pan. Mix it with the remaining oil. Return the shrimps and chicken to the pan. Mix and stir-fry them together with the "sauce" and with the cucumber and mushrooms for 1 minute. Sprinkle with sugar and soy sauce. Continue to stir-fry for ½ minute, and serve.

This is something of a party dish, and is extremely flavorsome.

Quick-fried Shrimps with Bean Sprouts and Ground Pork

2 tablespoons vegetable oil	2 tablespoons lard
1 tablespoon onion, finely chopped	2 tablespoons spring onion, in 1-inch segments
1 clove garlic, chopped	2 cups bean sprouts
½ cup ground or minced pork	1 tablespoon soy sauce
	3 tablespoons Broth
1 teaspoon salt	½ teaspoon Tabasco
1½ cups shrimp meat	3 tablespoons sherry

Heat oil in a frying pan. Add onion and garlic to stir-fry for ½ minute over high heat. Add pork and half the salt and stir-fry together for 2 minutes. Add shrimps and stir-fry together for 2 minutes. Remove with perforated spoon and keep hot.

Add lard to the pan. When it has melted add the spring onion and bean sprouts. Stir-fry over high heat for 2 minutes. Return the shrimps and pork to the pan. Sprinkle with remaining salt, soy sauce, Broth, Tabasco and sherry. Continue to stir-fry over high heat for 1 minute, and serve.

Quick-fried Shrimps with Celery and Ground Pork

Repeat the preceding recipe, substituting celery (cut diagonally into 1½-inch pieces) for bean sprouts, but stir-fry them for 1 minute longer before returning shrimps and pork to the pan for the final assembly frying.

Shrimps can be cooked in the same manner with almost any kind of vegetable with similar success, except with the hard vegetables, such as broccoli, cauliflower, asparagus, etc.; these will have to be parboiled for 3 or 4 minutes and drained before adding them to the stir-frying. With soft vegetables, such as spinach, tomato, etc., one has only to follow exactly the procedure of the above recipe. In this way a dozen or more recipes can be prepared by simply varying the combinations. In consequence, shrimps and prawns are among the most popular not only of Chinese seafoods but of almost of any kind of food when a delicious savory dish is needed at a moment's notice.

Quick-fried Shrimps with Sweet Peppers in Hot Savory Sauce

2 sweet peppers
2 chili peppers (if unavailable, use 2 teaspoons Tabasco)
2 tablespoons vegetable oil
1 tablespoon finely chopped onion
1 clove garlic, finely chopped
1 cup fresh or frozen shrimp

1 tablespoon lard
½ teaspoon salt
1 tablespoon tomato sauce
2 tablespoons Meat Gravy Sauce
1 teaspoon sugar
2 teaspoons vinegar
1 tablespoon sherry

Cut sweet peppers to pieces the size of shrimps, chili peppers into shreds (discard pips).

Heat oil in a frying pan. Add onion and garlic, and stir-fry for ½ minute. Add shrimps and stir-fry for 1 minute. Remove and keep warm.

Add lard. When it has dissolved, add chili peppers and stir-fry over high heat for ¼ minute. Add sweet peppers and stir-fry together for 1½ minutes. Return the shrimps to the pan. Add all the other ingredients to the pan and continue to stir-fry together over high heat for 1 minute; serve, to be eaten immediately.

Toasted Shrimps

This is a very similar dish to Toasted Fish (see page 166).

1 cup shrimp meat	1 tablespoon cornstarch
2 eggs	4 slices bread
½ teaspoon salt	2 cups bread crumbs
1 tablespoon chopped spring onion	Oil for deep-fry
	Few springs of parsley

Chop and mince the shrimp meat. Beat eggs for ¼ minute with rotary whisk in a bowl. Add one-quarter of eggs, salt, spring onion and cornstarch to the chopped shrimps. Mix well into a consistent paste. Cut away the crusts from the bread and cut each slice into quarters.

Spread the shrimp paste heavily on each piece of bread. Spread half the bread crumbs evenly on a tray. Dip the pieces of shrimp-pasted bread quickly in the remainder of the beaten egg. Place it on the bread crumbs on the tray. Sprinkle heavily with remaining bread crumbs. When all the pieces of shrimp-pasted bread have been crumbed, deep-fry them four at a time for 2½ minutes in very hot oil. Drain and arrange them neatly on a well-heated dish. Decorate each piece of "shrimp toast" with a pinch of parsley, and serve. (An excellent item to serve as a canapé at a cocktail party.)

Shrimp Scrambled Omelet

Whether this is an egg dish or a shrimp dish depends upon the relative quantity of the two materials used. In this case a preponderance of shrimps will be used.

2 cups shrimp meat	4 tablespoons oil
1½ teaspoons salt	Pepper to taste
4 eggs	2 tablespoons sherry
2 tablespoons chopped chives	

Sprinkle and rub shrimps with half the salt. Beat eggs lightly with remaining salt and chives.

Heat oil in a frying pan. Add shrimps and stir-fry gently for 2 minutes. Pour in the eggs. Tilt the pan so that the eggs will flow evenly over the pan and shrimps. Keep the heat moderate. When three-quarters of the eggs have set, sprinkle the eggs and shrimps with a liberal amount of pepper and the sherry. Stir and scramble the eggs and shrimps lightly and serve on a well-heated dish; to be eaten immediately.

Phoenix-tail Shrimps

1 dozen fresh giant unshelled shrimps (or Pacific prawns)	1 tablespoon onion, finely chopped
½ teaspoon salt	1 clove garlic, crushed and chopped
1 egg	Oil for deep-fry
4 tablespoons flour	
4 tablespoons water	

Shell the shrimp, except for its tail. Sprinkle and rub lightly with salt. Blend egg, flour, water, onion and garlic into a smooth batter. Dip the body of the shrimp into the batter (leaving out the tail).

Heat oil in a deep-fryer. When very hot place 4 shrimps at a time in a wire basket and deep-fry for 2½ minutes. Repeat until all the shrimps are fried. Serve to be eaten immediately by holding on to its tail, which should by now have turned quite pink or red. Best eaten dipped in pepper-salt mix. (Another fine dish for a cocktail party.)

Drunken Shrimps

2 cups shrimp meat (must be very fresh)
3 teaspoons salt
2 cloves garlic, finely chopped
2 teaspoons ginger root, finely chopped
6 tablespoons sherry
1 tablespoon brandy or rum

1 teaspoon Tabasco
1 tablespoon soy sauce
Freshly milled black pepper to taste
3 teaspoons salad oil
1 tablespoon chopped parsley
1 tablespoon chopped chives

Wash shrimps thoroughly. Sprinkle and rub with salt, garlic, ginger and sherry. Place in a refrigerator to marinate for 3 hours. Turn over and marinate for another 3 hours.

Drain away the marinade completely. Sprinkle with brandy, Tabasco, soy sauce, pepper and oil. Work them into the shrimps with fingers. Arrange nicely on dish. Sprinkle with chopped parsley and chives and serve (an excellent item for an hors d'oeuvre).

Oysters

Oysters are never eaten raw in China, as we consider this a barbarous and dangerous practice. In Chinese cooking they are usually deep-fried, quick-fried or prefried and assembled with other food materials to enhance and vary their flavors. Unlike shrimps, oysters are a purely coastal delicacy. The following are some of the ways they are usually prepared and cooked.

Deep-fried Oysters

2 dozen oysters
2 teaspoons salt
Pepper to taste
1 medium-size onion, finely
  chopped

3 tablespoons sherry
1 tablespoon chopped chives
Oil for deep-fry

For batter:

1 egg
6 tablespoons flour

1 tablespoon self-rising flour
6 tablespoons water

Shell oysters. Sprinkle with salt, pepper, chopped onion and sherry. Season for 15 minutes, and discard marinade.

Beat egg lightly. Blend with flour and water into a light batter.

Heat oil in the deep-fryer. When very hot, dip oysters in batter and deep-fry, five or six at a time, for 2 minutes. Drain on paper towel. Arrange on a well-heated dish, sprinkle with chopped chives and serve.

Deep-fried Oysters in Wine Sediment Paste

Repeat the preceding recipe. When all the oysters have been deep-fried heat 4 tablespoons Wine Sediment Paste and 1½ tablespoons lard in a frying pan. When hot stir and mix them together for ¼ minute. Add all the deep-fried oysters, sprinkle with chives, turn them in the sauce for ¾ minute and serve.

Barbecued (or Roast) Oysters

In some parts of coastal China (such as Fukien) oysters are grown in sea beds stuck with forests of bamboo sticks. When in season they are harvested by simply pulling up the sticks, around which the oysters have grown or stuck in clusters. These "sticks" of oysters are then simply turned around and around over a charcoal brazier, becoming "barbecued oysters." As the oysters are cooked inside their shells, they will simply pop open and are eaten with the dips listed on the following page. For convenience in the West, where oysters do not grow on sticks, it is easiest to roast them.

2 dozen oysters

For dips:

> Soy-tomato dip (2 tablespoons soy sauce mixed with 2 tablespoons tomato sauce)
>
> Soy-Tabasco dip (3 tablespoons soy sauce with 2 teaspoons Tabasco)
>
> Soy-sherry-garlic dip (2 tablespoons soy sauce with 2 tablespoons sherry and 1 clove garlic, chopped)
>
> Lemon juice (squeeze from fresh lemon)
>
> Soy-vinegar-ginger dip (2 tablespoons each of soy sauce and vinegar, with 2 teaspoons chopped fresh ginger or dried ginger)

Clean oysters thoroughly. Place them on a roasting pan or large flat heatproof dish in a single layer. Insert the pan or dish in a preheated oven at 475 degrees for 10 to 12 minutes.

By that time most of the oysters, having been cooked in their own juice, will have popped open. The dish or pan is then brought directly to the dining table and placed on a mat where each diner, equipped with a spoon and fork, will take and eat one oyster at a time after dabbing it first with drops of various dips. When served in such a way people (including the author) have been known to consume a hundred oysters at one sitting without ill effect!

Quick-fried Oysters with Ground Pork and Mushrooms

2 tablespoons vegetable oil
1 tablespoon onion, finely
  chopped
1 clove garlic, finely chopped
½ teaspoon salt
1 dozen oysters, shelled
1 tablespoon lard
1 cup minced pork
6 mushrooms, medium or
  large, destemmed

6 dried mushrooms (optional
  but preferable: soak in ½
  cup hot water for 20 minutes, reserving liquor; destem)
1½ tablespoons soy sauce
2 tablespoons sherry
1 teaspoon Tabasco

Heat oil in a frying pan. Add onion and garlic and salt. Stir-fry for ½ minute. Pour in the oysters, and stir-fry together for 1 minute. Remove with perforated spoon and keep warm.

Add lard and pork to the pan. Stir-fry pork for 3 minutes over high heat. Add the mushrooms. Stir-fry them together with pork for another 1½ minutes. Pour in the soy sauce, sherry, Tabasco and 4 tablespoons of mushroom liquor. Return the oysters to the pan. Assemble-fry them together for ¾ minute and serve to be eaten immediately.

Quick-fried Oysters with Pork and Vegetables

Oysters, like shrimps, can be cooked with pork and a majority of vegetables (such as broccoli, cauliflower, greens, spinach, celery, etc.) in the same manner as with mushrooms in the previous recipe. With fresh vegetables, as with fresh mush-rooms, no soaking is required, except with the hard vegetables, for which 3 to 5 minutes of parboiling may be required, and, of course, they will have to be cut into inch-square flat slices, or broken into individual branches, before adding to the pan.

16

Vegetables

CHINESE VEGETABLE DISHES are exceptionally tasty, mainly because of the cross-blending of flavors, which gives them richness of taste without distracting from their freshness. As we have already seen, a majority of meat and poultry dishes are mixed dishes cooked with a large percentage of vegetables. Except for the vegetarian ones, most Chinese vegetable dishes are cooked with meat broths or contain some element of meat. The principal sauces and ingredients which should be kept in readiness when cooking vegetable dishes are Gunpowder Sauce, Meat Gravy Sauce, Broth, Sweet and Sour Sauce. (See Chapter 3.) In addition fresh vegetables are often made more piquant by cooking them with dried, salted or pickled vegetables, as well as strong-flavored ones — such as pickles, chutneys, capers, ginger root (or dried ginger but not powdered), garlic, onion, dried mushrooms. These are often cooked in oil first, and then the bulk vegetables are in turn added and cooked in the flavor-impregnated oil. Meats and seafoods (dried shrimps, oysters, dried scallops) are often added. Because of this wide range of cross-cooking and cross-flavoring there are countless Chinese vegetable dishes. To give balance to a meal there should be at least one vegetable dish to every three of meat, fish, poultry or made-up combination.

Vegetables do not usually require prolonged cooking — the majority are produced in a matter of minutes. Dishes are classified in China as vegetable dishes if they have a preponderance of vegetables.

Plain Fried Spinach

1 pound spinach
4 tablespoons vegetable oil
2 tablespoons onion, finely chopped
1 clove garlic, finely chopped
½ tablespoon ginger (root or dried) shredded, if available

1 tablespoon chopped mixed pickles
1 teaspoon salt
4 tablespoons Meat Gravy Sauce
2 teaspoons sugar

Clean and drain spinach thoroughly, discarding coarser parts.

Heat oil in a large saucepan. Add onion, garlic, ginger, pickles. Stir-fry over high heat for ½ minute and add spinach and salt. Stir and turn the vegetable in the hot, flavor-impregnated oil for 2½ minutes. Add Meat Gravy Sauce and sugar, and continue to stir-fry over high heat for 2 to 2½ minutes and serve. One crushed chicken stock cube may be substituted for Meat Gravy Sauce.

Stir-fried Spinach with Shrimps

Repeat the preceding recipe, adding 4 to 6 tablespoons fresh shrimps a fraction of a moment before adding the spinach to the pan for the stir-fry. Thus the shrimp taste will impregnate the oil, which will in turn impregnate the spinach.

Spinach and Spaghetti Garnished with Shredded Ham

The preceding two dishes are meant as one of three or four dishes served at a full sit-down meal, but the present recipe should make a highly nutritious but economical dish for a self-contained snack for three:

Proceed as in either of the two preceding recipes. Meanwhile, parboil ¾ pound spaghetti for 17 to 18 minutes, and drain. When the spinach is ready and cooked in the saucepan, pour in the spaghetti and add 2 tablespoons butter and 6 tablespoons additional Meat Gravy Sauce. Stir and toss over low heat until the spaghetti and spinach are well distributed throughout. Shred 3 slices of ham (½ cup when shredded). Pour the spinach-spaghetti out on a large well-heated dish, or into 3 bowls. Garnish with shredded ham and serve.

Quick-fried Spinach with Red-cooked Meat

Repeat recipe for Plain Fried Spinach. When the spinach is ready, use it as the bed in a round or oval deep-sided dish. Pour 1 to 1½ pounds Red-cooked Beef or Red-cooked Pork on top in the center of the dish. The contrast between the glistening green of spinach and the rich brown of the beef or pork make it a very appealing dish.

Quick-fried Spinach with Pork and Mushrooms

The basic method employed here is to stir-fry the spinach and pork-and-mushrooms separately, and combine them in an assembly-frying for 1 minute before serving. The spinach should be cooked as in Plain Fried Spinach and ¼ pound pork should be sliced thin into 2-by-1-inch thin pieces, and stir-fried in oil (2 tablespoons) with 6 to 8 mushrooms (destemmed) and Gunpowder Sauce (2 tablespoons) for 3 minutes before they are added to the spinach for a final assembly-fry together, when a couple of tablespoons of sherry and a pinch of salt and pepper may be added; and if dried mushrooms are used, add 3 to 4 tablespoons liquor (derived from soaking them in hot water for 20 to 30 minutes).

Vegetarian Quick-fried Spinach

Repeat recipe for Plain Fried Spinach. Substitute Gunpowder Sauce for Meat Gravy Sauce, and add 6 to 8 mushrooms (preferably dried) together with 4 to 6 tablespoons mushroom liquor and 2 tablespoons sherry to the final stir-fry — which should be about 3 minutes over high heat.

Red-cooked Cabbage

1 medium-size cabbage (savoy or Chinese celery)	2 teaspoons sugar
3 tablespoons vegetable oil	1 teaspoon Tabasco
1 medium-size onion, chopped	6 tablespoons Meat Gravy Sauce (use Gunpowder Sauce if vegetarian)
1 clove garlic, chopped	
1 teaspoon salt	2 tablespoons sherry
1 tablespoon butter	

Chop cabbage into 2-by-1-inch pieces, discarding coarser leaves and base.

Heat oil in a large saucepan. Add onion and garlic. Stir-fry for ½ minute, add the cabbage. Sprinkle with salt; turn and stir the cabbage so that it is all well lubricated with oil. After 2 minutes of slow stir-frying, add butter, sugar, Tabasco, Meat Gravy Sauce and sherry. Continue to stir-fry for 2 minutes. Lower the heat to low-moderate and close the lid of the saucepan. Allow the contents to cook under cover for 4 to 5 minutes. Open the lid, give the cabbage a last turnover and serve — either in a bowl or a large deep-sided dish. In more elaborate cooking half a dozen soaked dried mushrooms (together with 3 to 4 tablespoons of mushroom liquor) are added in the braising, which will prolong the cooking time by 1 minute.

White-cooked Cabbage

Prepare the cabbage, and cook with the same initial ingredients as in the preceding recipe, but in the second stage of cooking, for Meat Gravy Sauce substitute 6 tablespoons Broth, ½ chicken stock cube, 6 tablespoons Fu Yung Sauce, 1 tablespoon butter and 1 teaspoon salt.

After the mixing and stirring, allow the mixture to cook under cover over low–moderate heat for 6 to 7 minutes, and wind up by sprinkling the cabbage with pepper (to taste) and 2 tablespoons sherry for a final half-minute stir-fry before serving in a bowl or deep-sided dish.

In the slightly more elaborate cases, 2 to 3 tablespoons of minced or chopped ham are used to sprinkle as garnish on the cabbage.

The above two cabbage dishes are classical ways in which Chinese cabbage is cooked, and are very popular among both rich and poor. The majority of Westerners have also found them extremely appealing. Like many Chinese vegetable dishes they can be eaten on their own or used as "starters," although with Chinese food they are normally served mainly to balance and complement meat and made-up dishes.

Cabbage with Meat-topped Noodles

For quick meals, which are self-contained and highly satisfactory, 2 or 3 cups of hot boiled spaghetti or egg noodles can be added to either of the above two dishes, and topped with a cup or two of Red-cooked Beef or Red-cooked Pork.

In Chinese households, where red-cooked meats and cooked cabbage (red or white) are, as I have mentioned, often available in the refrigerator or pantry, this dish can be made ready for serving in exactly the time required to boil the noodles or spaghetti, since it takes hardly any time at all to heat up the meat and cabbage.

Cabbage with Shrimp-topped (or Oyster-topped) Noodles

Repeat the preceding recipe, using any one of the shrimp or oyster dishes to top the noodles and vegetables (see Chapter 15).

As the seafood has to be freshly cooked, these dishes are more labor-consuming than the previous two, but for a one-dish meal they can be highly palatable and appealing.

Quick-fried Cabbage (*or Celery*) *in Sweet and Sour Sauce*

3 cups cabbage or celery
1 cup lean pork (optional)
3 tablespoons vegetable oil
1 tablespoon onion, finely
  chopped

1 clove garlic, chopped
1 teaspoon salt
4 to 6 tablespoons Sweet and
  Sour Sauce
3 tablespoons Broth

Slice cabbage in 1½-by-¾-inch pieces; or slice celery diagonally. Shred pork (if used) into thin strips. Heat oil in a saucepan or large frying pan. Add onion, garlic, pork and salt, and stir-fry together for 2 minutes over high heat. Add cabbage and continue to stir-fry for 5 minutes. Add Sweet and Sour Sauce and Broth for a further 2 minutes over high heat, and serve. This dish can be eaten hot or cold.

Bean Sprouts Quick-fried with Shredded Pork

1 cup lean pork
3 tablespoons vegetable oil
1 tablespoon onion, finely
  chopped
1 clove garlic, chopped

1 teaspoon salt
3 cups bean sprouts
1½ tablespoons soy sauce
3 tablespoons Broth
1 tablespoon vinegar

Shred pork into thin strips. Heat oil in a saucepan or large frying pan. Add onion, garlic, pork and salt and stir-fry together for 3 minutes over high heat. Pour in the bean sprouts. Turn and stir-fry with pork and oil for 1½ minutes. Add soy sauce, Broth and vinegar, continue to stir-fry for 1½ minutes and serve, to be eaten immediately.

Sliced Celery Quick-fried with Shredded Pork

Repeat preceding recipe substituting 2½ cups sliced celery
(sliced diagonally to ¼-inch thickness) for bean sprouts.
Otherwise, follow the same procedure, except 4 tablespoons
Meat Gravy Sauce should be added instead of soy sauce, and
the final stages of stir-frying should be extended to 2½ minutes. This will help in softening the celery, which is a harder
vegetable than bean sprouts.

Red- or White-cooked Celery

In Chinese cooking celery is considered a type of vegetable
similar to cabbage (the Chinese variety has a similar texture).
It can, therefore, be red-cooked or white-cooked in much the
same manner, by simply repeating the recipes for Red-cooked
Cabbage and White-cooked Cabbage — except with celery a
minute or two longer cooking will be required, and the addition of a couple of tablespoons of soaked dried mushrooms
(shredded) and soaked dried shrimps (if available) will be an
asset. These should be added at the same time as when the
bulk of the vegetable is added. In Western concept Red-
cooked Celery or White-cooked Celery can very well be
termed Red-braised or White-braised and can be eaten with
the main dish or served as a separate course.

Quick-fried White-braised Cauliflower (*or Pea Pods*)

1 large cauliflower or about 1
   pound pea pods
3 tablespoons vegetable oil
1 clove garlic, crushed
1 onion, finely chopped
1 teaspoon salt

Pepper to taste
¼ cup Broth
1 chicken stock cube, crushed
2 tablespoons sherry
2 tablespoons chopped ham or
1 teaspoon paprika

Clean and cut or break cauliflower into individual branches or flowerets, discarding coarse parts, or wash and trim pea pods.

Heat oil in a saucepan. Add garlic and onion and stir-fry over high heat for ¼ minute. Add cauliflower or pea pods, sprinkle with salt and pepper and turn in the hot oil for 2 minutes. Add Broth and stock cube; sprinkle with sherry. Turn the vegetables over once in the sauce, and close the lid of the saucepan. Cook under cover for 5 minutes. Pour the cauliflower and sauce into a deep-sided dish. Sprinkle with chopped ham and serve (if vegetarian, sprinkle with paprika).

Quick-fried Hot-braised Broccoli Topped with Crabmeat

For garnish:

3 to 5 tablespoons crabmeat
1½ tablespoons oil
1 clove garlic, crushed

½ tablespoon spring onion,
   chopped

Treat broccoli precisely as cauliflower is treated in the preceding recipe, except to omit garlic in first stir-fry, and to add 1 teaspoon Tabasco along with the Broth. In the garnishing, the crabmeat should be fried in oil with garlic and spring onion for 1 minute over high heat.

Quick-fried Broccoli or Cauliflower in Fu Yung Sauce

To produce a dish of broccoli or cauliflower in Fu Yung Sauce, proceed exactly according to either of the two preceding recipes, and add 6 tablespoons Fu Yung Sauce for ¾ minute slow stir-fry or folding in, before garnishing with ham or crabmeat, as the case may be, for serving.

Quick-fried Braised Lettuce or Pea Pods

2 heads lettuce or pea pods (about ¾ to 1 pound)	4 tablespoons Broth
2 tablespoons butter	1 tablespoon cornstarch, blended with 2 tablespoons
1 teaspoon salt	water and 2 tablespoons
½ chicken stock cube	sherry
2 tablespoons shredded ham	

Clean and cut off the roots of the lettuce, and leave the vegetable in full-length leaves, or wash and trim pea pods.

Heat butter in a frying pan. When it has melted, turn the lettuce in the butter, sprinkle with salt and crushed stock cube, for 2½ minutes over moderate heat. Sprinkle with shredded ham and pour in the Broth. Leave it to cook for 2 minutes. Turn the vegetable over a couple of times. Pour in the cornstarch-water-sherry mixture. Turn the vegetable over a couple more times in the thickened sauce, which should now be translucent. Serve, to be eaten immediately; to accompany browner and richer dishes.

Quick-fried Leeks or Sweet Peppers with Shredded Beef

Both leeks and sweet peppers are strong-flavored vegetables. They are seldom cooked and eaten on their own. More often than not they are cooked together with a strong-flavored meat, such as beef or lamb (even though a small amount of the meat).

¾ pound leeks, or 3 medium-size peppers
2 tablespoons butter
1 teaspoon salt
1 tablespoon oil
½ cup beef, shredded into thin strips

1 clove garlic, chopped
1 teaspoon sugar
1 tablespoon soy sauce
3 tablespoons Broth
½ teaspoon Tabasco
1 tablespoon sherry

Clean and cut leeks or peppers into approximately 1½-by-¾-inch pieces.

Heat butter in a large frying pan. Add leeks or peppers, sprinkle with salt, and stir-fry for 2 minutes over moderate heat. Remove from heat. Heat oil in a small frying pan. Add shredded beef and garlic; sprinkle with sugar and soy sauce; stir-fry over high heat for 1 minute. Add the beef to the large frying pan with Broth. Tabasco and sherry. Turn and stir-fry with leeks (or peppers) over high heat for 1¼ minutes. Serve, to be eaten immediately.

Casserole of Cabbage and Brussels Sprouts with Pig's Trotters

2 pairs of pig's trotters (approximately 1½ to 2 pounds)
1 cabbage (approximately 1½ to 2 pounds)
2 teaspoons salt
4 cups water

1 cup Broth
½ cup sherry
1 chicken stock cube
2 tablespoons chopped onion
1 pound Brussels sprouts, quartered; discard coarse leaves

Clean and parboil the trotters for 3 minutes. Drain and place at the bottom of a large casserole. Removing stem, cut cabbage vertically into 8 pieces. Place them over and around the trotters. Sprinkle with salt and pour in the water. Place the casserole in a preheated oven at 425 degrees. Heat for 10 minutes and reduce to 325 degrees. Leave to cook for 2 hours under cover. Open the lid, add Broth, sherry, stock cube, onion and the sprouts. Replace the lid of the casserole and return it to the oven to cook for another hour at 325 degrees. Serve in the casserole. (This semi-soup dish, with a large quantity of vegetables, is a boon to eat with rice. It is meant to stay on the table to be helped from throughout the meal.)

Casserole of Cabbage and Brussels Sprouts with Squabs

Repeat the preceding recipe, substituting squabs for trotters. The initial cooking, however, can be reduced by 1 hour. After cooking with the squabs buried under the cabbage, instead of adding Broth and sherry, substitute a red wine and add 2 tablespoons soy sauce along with sprouts. The dish from then on will only require one more hour of cooking in the oven at 325 degrees. Serve in the casserole. The meat of the squab, as in the previous recipe the meat of the trotters, is usually consumed along with the bulk of the vegetables.

Casserole of Celery and Watercress with Eel

1 ½ to 2 pounds eel
  2 bunches of water cress (ap-
    proximately ¼ pound)
  3 slices bacon
  1 clove garlic, crushed
  1 onion, chopped
3 ½ to 4 cups celery, cut into
  2-inch lengths

1 cup water
2 teaspoons salt
1 cup Broth
¼ cup sherry
1 ½ tablespoons soy sauce

Chop eel into 2-inch segments. Parboil for 3 minutes and drain. Clean watercress and cut away the muddier stems.

Lay the bacon at the bottom of the casserole and lay the pieces of eel on top. Add garlic and onion. Cover them with celery. Pour in the water and sprinkle with salt. Place the casserole in a preheated oven at 425 degrees for 15 minutes. Reduce to 325 degrees and cook for ½ hour. Add watercress, Broth, sherry and soy sauce. Return the casserole into the oven, heat under cover at same temperature for another 45 minutes and serve in casserole.

Casserole of Leeks and Cabbage with Lamb Chops

1½ pounds lamb chops
  1 clove garlic, crushed
1½ pounds cabbage (approxi-
    mately 3 to 4 cups cut to
    2-inch pieces)
  1 pound leeks

2 cups water
2 teaspoons salt
1 cup Broth
1 cup sherry
2 tablespoons soy sauce

Place the lamb chops at the bottom of a casserole. Add garlic and cover with cabbage and leeks. Pour in the water and sprinkle with salt. Place in oven at 425 degrees for 15 minutes and reduce to 350 degrees for 1 hour. Open the lid of casserole, add Broth and sherry and adjust seasoning with soy sauce. Heat for another ¾ hour and serve in the casserole. (This is another favorite semi-soup dish, which is eaten throughout the meal, starting with eating the vegetables and ending by drinking the soup, and consuming all the meat from the chops, which should now be very tender.)

Steamed Vegetable Bowl

1 to 1½ pounds squash	6 dried mushrooms (optional
3 hearts of spring greens	but desirable)
1 small cabbage	6 large mushrooms
½ pound spinach	2 tablespoons butter
1 bundle watercress	1½ tablespoons soy sauce
2 teaspoons salt	1 teaspoon sugar
2 cups Broth	4 tablespoons sherry

This dish should only be attempted if you have a steamer or a large boiler in which a very large deep-sided dish, containing the vegetables, can be conveniently placed on a rack or raised platform, and 1½ to 2 inches of water in the boiler can be kept at a rolling boil without splashing into the dish or bowl containing the vegetables.

Cut the squash into 4-by-2-inch pieces after removing the tough skin. Cut each heart of green vertically in two. Stand the squash pieces and hearts of green around the wall of the deep-sided dish. Fill up the well in the middle with chopped cabbage (2-by-1-inch pieces), spinach which has been thoroughly cleaned, and watercress (with white roots removed). Sprinkle with salt and pour in the Broth.

Meanwhile, soak the dried mushrooms (if available) for 20 minutes and remove stems. The fresh mushrooms should also be thoroughly cleaned and stems removed. Heat butter in a frying pan. When it has melted, add the mushrooms and stir-fry for 1 minute. Add soy sauce and sugar, and stir-fry for a further minute. Pile the mushrooms on top of the watercress at the center of the vegetable dish. Pour the remaining butter and gravy from the pan over the mushrooms. Place the dish in the steamer, or on a raised platform in the cauldron or boiler, and steam vigorously for ½ hour. Add sherry and adjust for seasoning; continue to steam for 15 minutes more and bring the dish directly from the steamer to serve on the table.

Chinese Salad

The Chinese salad differs from the average Western salad only in the composition of the dressing. We use soy sauce, concentrated Broth, sesame oil, ginger root, sherry. Sesame oil is used only for flavoring, and therefore, only a very small amount is used. Ginger root has a very distinctive taste to contribute, but if not available use chopped lemon-rind shavings. Where available also use chopped coriander, which contributes a memorable and unmistakable flavor.

The dressing can be applied to a majority of salads or combinations of raw vegetables, such as:

Lettuce, shredded cabbage, sliced cucumber, celery, celeriac, radishes, tomatoes, chicory, etc. Some hard vegetables, such as carrots, cauliflower and broccoli, can also be used successfully in salads if parboiled for 3 to 4 minutes first.

For dressing:

3 tablespoons soy sauce
½ teaspoon salt
4 tablespoons concentrated
　Broth (melt ¼ chicken stock
　cube in 4 tablespoons Broth)
1 teaspoon chopped ginger
　root (or 2 teaspoons
　chopped lemon rind)
1 clove garlic, chopped
2 tablespoons sherry

2 tablespoons wine vinegar
½ teaspoon Tabasco
2 teaspoons sugar
Pepper to taste
4 tablespoons salad oil
2 teaspoons sesame oil
2 teaspoons chopped chives
1 tablespoon chopped
　coriander (if available)

The combination of the above ingredients should make sufficient dressing for a very large bowl of vegetables (2 to 3 pounds).

The presence of sesame oil, soy sauce, ginger and concentrated Broth should give it a very distinctive and appealing flavor.

17

Sweets

THERE ARE FEW SWEETS in China which can be said to make much of a contribution to the world of desserts when compared with the more sophisticated range of this type of foods in the West. There are, however, a few categories of Chinese sweets which, because of their difference in approach and concept, might prove intriguing and appealing and which do not require too elaborate a process to prepare.

Almond Curd (or Jelly)

The Chinese almond curd or jelly consists mainly of a jelly made out of finely ground almond with milk, sweetened water and gelatin or agar. When the jelly is set cut it into ½-inch cubes or diamond shapes and serve them in syrup. The significant contribution here is the introduction of nutty flavor to sweetened fruit dishes.

If almonds can be used so can walnuts, chestnuts or even peanuts. When the powdered nuts have been jellied and cut into cubes and diamonds, they can be served with different combinations of fruits in fruit salads.

Almond Curd

2 cups almond meat
2 cups water
4 tablespoons sugar
1 cup evaporated milk

1 to 1½ envelopes gelatin
    dissolved in ½ cup water
½ tablespoon almond extract

Grind and blend almond into a smooth paste in a mixer, with water. Filter through double cheesecloth into a bowl. Add sugar, stir to dissolve.

Heat evaporated milk in a saucepan. Add almond mixture and finally stir in the dissolved gelatin. Add almond extract. Stir slowly until ingredients are well blended.

Pour the mixture into a shallow dish to cool. When cool place in a refrigerator to set. When the curd or jelly is well set, cut it into half-inch cubes or diamond shapes. They can be served in any combination of salad or fruit cocktail.

As I have said, what can be done with almonds can also be done with walnuts, chestnuts or even peanuts — simply by grinding and blending them into a smooth cream and making them into rich nut-flavored jellies.

Glazed Fruits

The best known of these glazed fruits is the Glazed Apple, which in its essence consists of cut pieces of apple dipped into hot molten sugar, and then the apple section is dipped momentarily into a bowl of ice water to chill its molten sugar coating into a brittle crust. The crust cracks readily when bitten into. This provides both an interesting sensation and a sharp taste of sweetness, which are especially welcomed after a savory meal. In Peking it is called Silk Thread Apple because of the long glasslike threads the apples draw when removed and pulled away from the molten sugar.

Glazed Silk Thread Apples

3 to 4 crisp apples

For batter:

1 egg	1 cup flour
½ cup water	Oil for deep-fry

For glazing syrup:

4 tablespoons peanut oil	1 tablespoon honey
5 tablespoons sugar	

Core the apples and cut each into 8 pieces. Mix the ingredients for batter into a smooth mixture. Dip apple into batter, divide into 3 lots and deep-fry each lot for 2½ minutes. Drain on paper toweling.

Heat the ingredients for the syrup mixture in a saucepan (oil first). Stir and heat gently until ingredients have formed into a thick consistent syrup. Dip the apples in the syrup. Drain or pull them out quickly and give them a quick dip in a large bowl of ice water. Withdraw immediately, and let them drain on each diner's plate. When they are cool the diner will find the pieces of apple extremely sweet and crackling and interesting to bite into.

What can be done with apples here can also be done with other fruits with similar texture, such as peaches, pears or even with bananas, another favorite fruit which is often prepared in this manner.

Steamed Pears

Steamed Pears is another generic form of Chinese hot fruit dish served as dessert. What can be done with pears can again be done with other fruits of similar shape, size and texture — apples, peaches, etc.

6 pears

2 cups of sugar water (4 tablespoons sugar dissolved in 2 cups water)

3 tablespoons powdered sugar

6 teaspoons kirsch, or any suitable liqueur (fruit brandies, crème de menthe)

Peel the pears neatly, except for the part immediately surrounding the stalk (keep stalk). Slice ¼-inch off the bottoms to flatten them, so that they will stand firmly. Arrange the 6 pears upright on a flat-bottom, deep-sided heatproof dish. Pour in the sugar water. Place the dish in a steamer, or on a raised platform mounted in a large boiler. Steam steadily for 30 to 35 minutes. Remove the dish from the boiler. Sprinkle the pears with sugar and liqueur. Allow them to cool for 10 to 15 minutes and then place the dish in a refrigerator to chill for 2 hours.

When serving place the pears in 6 individual serving bowls or cups. Pour some of the syrup in the dish over each pear.

In the more elaborate versions, if time is of little consideration, the top half-inch of each pear can be cut off as a lid with stalk attached, and the fruit is carefully cored halfway through. The cavity of the core is then stuffed or filled with what you like: cinnamon-flavored honey, nuts, other fruits. The pears are then steamed with lids on. When they are ready the peeled pears can be painted with artificial food coloring before sprinkling with sugar and liqueur.

Miniature Ice-Mountains

Another Chinese custom in serving peeled fruits is to sprinkle or dip them in sugar. In the present case, the peeled fruit (chopped to somewhat larger size than normally used in fruit salads or cocktails) is covered with a pile of chipped ice, and then sprinkled with colored sugar.

4 bowls fruit salad, coarsely
chopped
2 cups chipped ice (as dry
as possible)
4 teaspoons liqueur (kirsch,

cherry brandy, crème de
menthe, etc.)
4 tablespoons multicolored
"rainbow" sugar

Place the fruit salad in the refrigerator to chill for one hour. Prepare the chipped ice ten minutes before serving. Place the latter in freezer to chill and dry.

When ready to serve, pour and pile ¼ cup of chipped ice on top of the center of each bowl of fruit salad, sprinkle with liqueur and multicolored sugar and serve.

Chipped ice so treated has the quality of water ice, and the touch of liqueur provides just that additional refreshing impact. This dessert follows a Chinese tradition, but is served in a way which is more suitable to Western usage. In Peking it is served on a large dish, using chipped ice as a bed, and with individual dishes of sugar strategically placed as dips. The pieces of fruits are picked up, dipped and eaten with chopsticks.

INDEX

Index

Quick-fried Sweet Peppers with Shredded Beef, 206–207
Quick-fried White-braised Cauliflower, 204
quick-frying. *See* stir-frying
quick-stir-frying. *See* stir-frying

Red-cooked Cabbage, 199–200
Red-cooked Chicken, 123
Red-cooked Fish
  Steaks, 150–151
  (whole), 148–149
  (whole) Garnished with Ham and Vegetables, 149–150
Red-cooked Lamb, 97
Red-cooked Pork, 67–72
  Basic, 67–68
  with Chestnuts, 69
  Chopped, with Abalone, 70
  Chopped, with Carrots, 70
  Chopped, with Chestnuts, 71
  Chopped, with Potatoes, 71
  Chopped, with Salted Fish and Anchovy, 70
  with Eggs, 68
  Spareribs, 71–72
  with Spinach, 68–69
Red- or White-cooked Celery, 203
Rice, 42–49
  Boiled, 42–43
  Fried, 43–46
  Meat Fried, 45
  Seafood Fried, 45–46
  Topped, with Diced Chicken, Mushrooms and Frozen Peas, 48
  Topped, with Sliced Soy Steak and Broccoli, 47–48
  Topped, with Sweet and Sour Pork and Fu Yung Cauliflower, 49
  Vegetable Fried, 44–45
root ginger. *See* ginger root

sauces, 13–17
  Fu Yung (White Sauce), 14–15
  Gunpowder, 13
  Meat Gravy, 14

sauces (*contd.*)
  Plum, 17
  soy, 1
  Sweet and Sour, 15–16
scallion. *See* spring onion
Scallops, 178–179, 180–183
Scrambled Omelet with Sweet and Sour Sauce, 141
Seafood Fried Rice, 45–46
seasonings, 1–2, 6–7
Shellfish, 168–194
  See also Abalone, Clams, Crabs, Lobsters, Oysters, Scallops, Shrimp(s)
sherry, 2, 6
Shredded Chicken, 107–109
  with Celery, 108
  Quick-fried with Bean Sprouts, 107
  Quick-fried with Shredded Mushrooms and Bamboo Shoots, 108
  with Sweet Pepper and Chili Pepper Ribbons, 109
Shredded Duck, 133
Shrimp(s), 178–189
  Drunken, 189
  Dry-fried, 179–180
  Phoenix-tail, 188–189
  Scrambled Omelet, 188
  Stir-fried "Phoenix" and "Dragon," 184
  Toasted, 187
  See also Quick-fried Shrimps
Shrimps and Peas in White Soup, 41
Simplified Broth, 13
Sliced Beef
  with Tomato and Egg-flower Soup, 32
  with Watercress Soup, 31–32
Sliced Celery Quick-fried with Shredded Pork, 203
Sliced Chicken, 109–112
  Quick-fried with Broccoli, 110
  Quick-fried with Cauliflower, 109–110
  Quick-fried with Mushrooms, 110–111

Stir-fried Pork (*contd.*)
  Sliced, with Mushrooms and Dried
    Mushrooms, 80
Stir-fried Spinach with Shrimps, 197
stir-frying, 4, 5–8
Stuffed Deep-fried Clams, 172
Stuffed Fish Simmered in Wine and
  Vinegar Sauce, 162–163
Stuffed Sweet Peppers, 82
Suggested Menus, 19, 20–28
Superior Broth, 12
Sweet Peppers, Quick-fried, with
  Shredded Beef, 206–207
Sweet and Sour Carp, 153–154
Sweet and Sour Pork, 76
Sweet and Sour Sauce, 15–16
Sweets, 213–218

Tabasco, 2
times, for food preparation and
  cooking, 9–11
Toasted Shrimps, 187
tomato purée, 2
tomato sauce, 2
Topped Rice, 46–49
  with Diced Chicken, Mushrooms
    and Frozen Peas, 48
  with Sliced Soy Steak and Broc-
    coli, 47–48
  with Sweet and Sour Pork and Fu
    Yung Cauliflower, 49
Topped and Scrambled Noodles
  with Beef-tomato Sauce, 64
  with Piquant Meat Sauce, 63–64
  with Shredded Chicken and Ham
    and Parsley Dressing, 62
  with Shredded Duck and Mustard
    Sauce, 61–62
  with Vegetarian Dressings, 64–65
Triple-layer Scrambled Omelet with
  Shrimps, 139–140

Triple-shred Soup, 34
Twice-cooked Pork, 75

Vegetable Fried Rice, 44–45
Vegetable Soup, 40
Vegetables, 7, 195–212
  Chinese Salad, 211–212
  Steamed, 210–211
  See also Cauliflower, Spinach, etc.
Vegetarian Dressings, 64–65
Vegetarian Quick-fried Spinach, 199
Vegetarian Scrambled Omelet, 141
Vermicelli. *See* Noodles

White Fish and Green Pea Soup, 37
White Fish and Spring Green Soup,
  36
White Sauce. *See* Fu Yung Sauce
White-cooked Cabbage, 200–201
White-cooked Pork, 72–73
  Chopped, with Abalone and Cab-
    bage, 73
  Chopped, with Ham, 72
  in whole piece, 73
White-cut Chicken, 116–117
wines, to serve, 21–22
Wine Sediment Paste, 16–17
  Chopped Braised-fried Chicken in,
    115
  Chopped Dry-fried Duck in, 132–
    133
  Deep-fried Oysters in, 191
  Fish Steaks in, 152–153
  Quick-fried Scallops with, 180
  Quick-fried Shrimps with, 181
  Sliced Fish Quick-fried in, 167
  Stewed Lamb in, 97
  with Triple-quick-fries, 96–97
Wine-simmered Duck, 135–136
wok, 3